MELANIN

Netta B.

Copyright © 2018 Netta B.

All rights reserved.

ISBN: 0-9862995-8-8
ISBN-13: 9780986299582

DEDICATION

"I ultimately always push people. There isn't anybody that knows me that can say they have told me something that they desired to do or even shared something positive and I did not amp them up in some fashion shape or form. I've always been that someone that's says "that sound dope" or "okay I can see you doing that". I'm always dropping a compliment here and there. The reason that I push people so hard or try to uplift them is because, I know what it's like to want to do something or carry a talent that you know you can accomplish. Something that you know you will enjoy in life, and not have that emotional or mental backing that extra needed push. A mothers love is sometimes just not enough, until one day you realize it is. Sometimes it's almost like people know you can do it so their just sitting and watching and waiting for you to get it done or to just fail, and it's so much of that energy around us. I have been a victim of hate so much that I really try and be that person that pushes. We all need some form of motivation, yea we can do it alone, and yes we can get it done ourselves. Something about that motivation. It gives you something to look forward to it pushes you to get the job executed. Now you are motivated to get the job done because you know hey somebody cares and believes in me. Someone is routing for me. That simple fact right there is how it gets better and your drive stronger. So that's all I'm trying to do I'm trying to push you because at the end of the day we all need it, all of us. And just because I haven't had that push I'm not going to deter or stop your dreams I'm going to hype you up…maybe that's my purpose. Maybe I don't have a million dollar dream or I can't give you a million dollars. Maybe my job is to just encourage you maybe to get blessed through my encouragements to somebody who knows? The point is, you all have to live. You have to live and let, let and live. Let all the positive good shit come your way absorb it sit in it, let all the bad negative shit go, walk away. Fuck it. LET and LIVE!" **Netta B.**

Have you ever opened a book only to find there were not enough black acknowledgements or images inside? That whatever it was that you just mentally devoured somehow made your depiction to be bad or almost feel victim like?

That's one reason I created this book. I wanted to see bundles of pages filled with straight struggles, encouragement, pain, determination, belief, which led or lead to accomplishments, perseverance, legacies but above all else color. So please don't think this book was made with ill intent, or made for growth of hate due to injustice or seeking reparations. Instead it was made with pride, heritage, knowledge and discoveries in mind. Welcome to a world where it's not either Black or White just BROWN. Enjoy!

> *"You go to school you study about the German and the French, not about your own race. I hope the time will come when you study Black History too."*
>
> *Booker T. Washington*

I dedicate this book to **YOU**, may it keep you encouraged.

> *"Give light and people will find the way."*
>
> *Ella Baker*

CONTENTS

1	Introduction	I
2	Honorable mentions	Pg. 7
3	This is just a test to see what you know	Pg. 30
4	Inventors/Inventions	Pg. 61
5	True or False	Pg. 84
6	Fun Facts	Pg. 97
7	Back in the Day	Pg. 126
8	Stumbled on the Internet	Pg. 159
9	This is so Cool to Me	Pg. 187
10	A Few Places to Visit	Pg. 202
11	Things you should know being a American Citizen	Pg. 215
12	Social, Charity, Educational, Self-help	Pg. 231
13	The Future is Bright	Pg. 246
14	Quotes, Speeches, Conversation	Pg. 252
15	Melanin Playlist	Pg. 353
16	Moment of Silence	Pg. 369
17	Final Thoughts	Pg. 378

MELANIN

DISCLAIMER

I do not claim every word of this book to be one thousand percent true nor a learning curriculum. What you are about to indulged in is produced from research via the internet and a couple of my own educated guesses and opinions. This is merely a stepping stone to provoke you to continue to learn and research to fully know and understand yourself by getting a grip and glimpse of your past so you confidently and unapologetically know and claim your future.

Some documents that were posted I felt were more vivid then words. The mind sometimes can't grasp what our eyes don't see.

I do not own the rights to any pictures.

Netta B.

Introduction

Hello young world and welcome to the world of Melanin. This particular book was bigger than me and I didn't do it for the fame or fortune but because I felt it was time. This vision came to me the beginning of 2017 a time I felt the world was becoming so unpredictable and unapologetically hateful while we as people seem so lost. So I wanted to celebrate us give hope and pride. I feel people of today are harsh and most times the black on black love even harsher. I wrote multiple things downs wondering how would I format and present this information not throwing it in faces but simply laying it out and making it available for people to either indulge or at least be receptive to what I believe people don't know, not because they don't care but because the world and media has laid out in front of us as to what they think is important. For months in the beginning I just wanted to present this info with a pseudonym that was not representative of me I didn't want my name to deter anyone from buying or even glimpsing through this book I also was going to name this book "Black", ehh. Later I said we are not just "Black" it's deeper than that and that's where "Melanin" came in at and second I remembered I want to be a best seller I want to write any and everything and it be great. That's what I will be known for, writing whether it is a book, article, movie, blog, play etc. if I wrote it I want my name attached. So whoop here it is! Young heads won't get that one. LOL.

By now I sure your probably asking what exactly is this book, what am I really about to read? I would consider this my Universal version of the Green Book written by Victor Hugo Green. In the Jim Crow Era Green created a book telling all Black Travelers what roads, city, and business that were Black business friendly mostly covering the North America area. That's kind of what I would like this to be to you a guide. I put a variety of things in this book on all different kind of subjects because black is beautiful, sad, strong, scary, peaceful, and most importantly it is us and we need to embrace it. So "Melanin" is our Spark Notes to the beginner's guide of Black, Moors, Aboriginal, Indigenous people history and culture.

I sometimes find myself talking about the youth. Our younger generation mainly feeling dejected so in my mind this is my way of helping and doing something to inspire them to do and be better. This is me I feel doing a little bit of my part. This was done selflessly and wanting to pass it on just to open someone's eyes. This is way bigger than me. This has nothing to do with me only to reach out to my long line of brothers and sisters second first tenth cousins just so they can run and tell their child or themselves don't believe everything that you hear and picture that you see. Sometimes you have to dig a little bit deeper sometimes you have to research, and that's the point of this book. Its purpose is for you to research. The point of this book is for you to learn, the point is for you to know, the point of this book is for you to dig within yourself and for you to find motivation and determination to do whatever it is that you want to do in life. You have to know that the past is just that the past. With that being said you have to understand and know the past to firmly grasp the future.

There are so many strong minded individuals your age, my age, a year old maybe two, and they haven't reached that level of certainty because someone hasn't pushed them told them that was brave or intelligent for that move. Maybe instead they may have heard shut up, sit down; your opinion doesn't matter even a little. All a person needs is one person one being to be like "Gone on now I see you baby!" Ask the youth what they like notice what their good at feed those interest. We have to do better with our youth stop giving them phones or tablets and sitting them in a corner. Put order in these children lives and stop letting them think they are grown. With that being said no this book is not for kids well not all of it I'll leave that up to the parents. When it comes down to it I don't think this is children reading material but it can be used as a tool of learning. For instance when they are younger you may not want to share everything in this book but rather maybe different stages in their life or you may just want to pick the book up let it be seen or maybe have them memorize a few quotes out of it or share some of the good things out of it like what such and such did and who such and such is or when something happened because at the end of the day that's what this all boils down to, it is really to show and teach the good things, obstacles and executions the belief and the desire to actually make a change. This isn't a book for everybody. This a book for certain age range at a certain level of maturity with an open mind set, a person in the reality of things verses the facade or keeping up with the masses. It's a tool you can have around and share and teach in pieces to a young child. This is for you to grow and expand and them to just have in their psyche and mind so when they can read comprehend and learn it'll be right there.

I know for me even though I know about a few ancestors, holidays, and events the issue is sometimes I forget and it is because unlike most "major" holidays I don't have reminders on that day to day or around that specific date. I don't have that reminder on television, radio, or billboards it is something you would have to just know ultimately something we have to build around us in order to remember embrace and live it you turn it into a lifestyle. I don't want you to just research I want you to explore and know I need this and hope it will influence you. Incorporate history, pictures, holidays, and quotes into your life so you and the people around you will not be so quick to forget. The world is not for us it loves us but it is not for us it's not a friendly environment. I mean just look at our society everything about it screams URBAN, swag this swag that even different genres of music have a soul feel to it now a days over in Asia they are us from dress hair music to getting our cars imported overseas to them. Maybe think about the emblems and symbols taken and used daily that we have no clue about like the legacy of General Hannibal, Phoenix and eagle on the American dollar bill, Heru and Auset, the swastika dates back 12,000 years to Ethiopia, why shoot the big nose off of monuments, Yemaya and starbucks, PTAH and the OSCARS trophy, and the list goes on.

Open your eyes and look around it's a reason. We are royalty a chosen race and everybody is aware of it except the majority of us. We need to and I believe we have the desire to come together that intuition that good that we really want to show and give its real but media won't let us.

Ninety nine percent of all names in this book are Black race and very much real and or relevant. Turn a page and discover.

So here we go, welcome to our show!

Melanin

From the Greek work Melas, Melan meaning black first used in the mid-19th century

A natural molecule or substance that gives color, life, and consciousness to every tree, plant, animal, mother earth and the universe, while connecting them with one another.

A dark brown or black pigment occurring in the hair, skin, and iris of the eye in people and animals. It is responsible for tanning of skin exposed to sunlight. – Oxford definition

Insoluble pigments that account for the color in skin, scales, and feathers. – Vocabulary.com definition

CARBON

Dark matter consciousness

~An absorber of light~

Netta B.

Honorable mentions

Okay, in this book of encouragement and acknowledgement I'm going to be starting off with a couple of people that we all most likely already know. Although throughout this entire book are names I believed are some valuable pieces needed to the puzzle. When I build a puzzle for some reason I don't know why but I've been doing it for years I build the boarder first and build my puzzle from outside going in. So in my eyes these people are the boarder of the puzzle or I guess what I believe to be the foundation... I say the border because I believe there is so much more to be done for us as a people and the puzzle may not be complete until someone possibly a young person picks this material up and finds something to motivate them. It could be a person born five to ten to however many years from now who just has the spirit and determination to do and make things better. These are names I think every child of any race should know. These are names of people who felt no fear or doubt about what they were doing or needed to be done. Knowing and understanding the consequences while still continuing to take control for their own destiny not just for themselves but for all.

These people believed that everyone deserved the joys and freedom of living, not just having life. They maybe believed people were tired hurt or just plain giving up. I believe they knew or just felt like that they had to make moves in order to see a change because everyone deserves a betterment but few actually move or pursue which leads to them not conquering. The only way to create change is to climb up and out of the box.

Some similar characteristics they shared were individuality, strength, faith, and love, for the human race in general but ultimately for self. In my opinion that is where anything truly begins. In order to be able to execute or master anything you have to know yourself as a person. You know why I believe white people are so proud? Because they have is a history that is etched in millions of writings. So if we accept our race, our black history, in general our own direct family history listening to ancestors stories too we can better guide ourselves and our descendant's future story.

So here are a few people who left marks in the world. I suggest you find and research these people, they have amazing back stories some doing a 360 of what they thought their future would bring, some not even realizing the impact they had on the world, and others knowing exactly what it was they wanted to stand for or their story opening doors or eyes.

Nat turner born October 2 1800-November 11,1831

was a enslaved African American who led a rebellion of slave and free blacks in Southampton county Virginia on August 21 1831 the rebels went from plantation to plantation taking horses and guns freeing slaves along the way and recruit free blacks on the way. As a result off the revolt around 55 whites were killed and 200 blacks were killed mostly innocent of the rebellion by white militant and around 50 black found guilty and charged. Also new laws were passed. Prohibited education of slaves and free blacks, restricted rights of assembly for free black, no rights to bear arms in some states and the right to vote were taken away, and also requiring a white minister to be present at all black worship services. Turner hid for two months after his rebellion but was found when a dog sniffed him out and was later hung to his death. Oct.2, 1800-Nov 11, 1831 he was hanged skinned then beheaded to frighten any want to be rebels. His body was buried and his skull passed around from hand to hand. In 2016 what is assumed to be his skull was returned to his descendants

Fredrick Douglas born Frederick Augustus Washington Bailey Feb. 1818- Feb. 20 1895 at the age of 77 due to a heart attack. He was an abolitionist, suffragist author editor preacher diplomat. Political party republican Douglas was a run a way slave from Maryland who took three attempts to see his freedom as a black man. A free black woman named Anna Murray was all the strength and help he needed on his last third attempt. On September 3, 1838 jumping on the Philadelphia Wilmington and Baltimore railroad reaching his freedom in less than 24 hr. Douglass was the only African American to attend the first women's rights convention The Seneca Falls Convention in 1848 standing to speak in favor.

Angela Davis Born Angela Yvonne Davis born on January 26, 1944. Davis is an author, American Political activist, and academic Scholar. Davis had deep ties with the Black Panther Party due to her involvement in the Civil Rights Movement, and was the leader of Communist Party USA. Davis also feels deep about feminism. If you further research Davis you will learn her story of why she became one of Americas most wanted she capture and her release. Davis is a movie waiting to be written if you ask me.

President Barak Obama born Barack Hussein Obama the second on August 4, 1961 Obama was the first African American President serving as number 44 alongside that great accomplishment he served two terms.

James Armistead was a double spy who helped with the battle of Richmond he wanted to help his home state so asked General Lafayette to help Lafayette sends him Benedict Arnold a general in the British army as a spy claiming the Americans were treating him so bad. Arnold liked Armistead influencing him to introduce him to other British Generals and they become really fond of Armistead asking him to be a spy on the Americans of course he agrees setting the bait and leading for the British into a trap where the French fleet quietly waited surrounded and conquered the British. He received or was granted his freedom.

Michelle Obama born Michelle LaVaugue Robinson Obama on January 17, 1964. Becoming the first African American First lady of the United States and represented the image of the Black queen well. Obama is a writer and lawyer. Her main focus for Americas was to focus on poverty awareness, nutrition, physical activity, and healthy eating.

Emmett Till born Emmett Louis Till on July 25, 1941- August 28-1955 Till was a teenage boy out visiting family in Mississippi. It is said several days after being in the city one day while playing checkers outside a store he whistled at a white woman who owned a store the woman's husband and brother in law kidnapped Till in the dead night beating him to mutilation and throwing him in a river. Days later his nude body that was weighed down by a gin mill iron fan was found by a fisherman and sent back to Chicago to his mother. Till's mother decided to have an open casket funeral displaying her son body to the world to show them what hate looks like. Till killers were acquitted later in a magazine interview Tills killers later admitted to the murder but was protected by double jeopardy laws. Because of how high profile volatile this case became a pivot point to the Civil Rights Movement. In 2007 Carolyn Bryant the woman Emmett Till exchanged words or gestures with admitted to fabricating her testimony in a book *The Blood of Emmett Till*.

Shirley Chisholm born Shirley Anita St. Hill Chisholm November 30 1924- January 1 2005 was an author, educator, and American politician. The first African

American women elected to the United States Congress. She was also the first black candidate for a major party nomination for president of the United States Chisholm is the first woman to run for Democratic Party presidential nomination.

Peter Salem fought alongside Thomas Grosvenor in the Battle of Bunker Hill 1817 Salem had 14 military commendations.

Sara Forbes Bonetta born Aina 1843-August 15, 1880 was a west African of Yoruba royalty who was orphaned and sold into slavery then somehow became the god daughter of Queen Victoria. She later married James Pinson Labulo Davies.

Thurgood Marshall born July 2 1908-January 24,1993 an associate justice of the Supreme Court of the United States the very first African American Justice and making the list of the first one hundred Justice list. He was also part of the third highest ranking official in the U.S. Department of Justice named a United States Solicitor General. Marshall was known for his role and victory as a lawyer in the Brown vs, Board of Education. If you research him you will find out that some of the slackers and pranksters untimely find their way.

Lena baker born June 8 1900-March 5 1945 only Women in the state of Georgia to be executed by electrocution in 2005 she was pardoned for her wrongful conviction. The movie "The Lena Baker Story" can give your insight.

Crispus Attucks born 1723- March 5,1770 Attucks is the first martyr to the cause of American Patriotism pegged to be the very first person killed in the Boston Massacre but widely referred to as the first African American Killed in the American Revolution.

Nancy green born November 17, 1834-September 23, 1923 cook, activist, storyteller, and model. Nancy Green was known as Aunt Jemima. Because of there being no paperwork or contracts written her family does not receive revenue. The way she passed always makes my mouth drop.

Joseph Hayne Rainey born June 21 1832 into slavery was the first African American to serve in the United States house of representative also being the second black person to serve in the United States congress a member of the Republican Party.

Hattie McDaniel born June 10, 1895 October 26, 1952 was an actress, singer, songwriter, and comedian. McDaniel has two stars on the Hollywood Walk of Fame one for radio and the other motion pictures. Best known for her work in "Gone with the Wind" she was the first African American to win an Academy Award of Best Supporting Actress.

Oscar Micheaux born Oscar Devereaux Micheaux January 2,1884-March 25,1951 first African American independent producer, writer and director of over 40 films.

Sister Rosetta Thorpe born March 20 1915- October 9, 1973 was a songwriter, singer, recording artist and guitarist "the original soul sister' and "godmother of soul" you may know her for her 1944 hit "Down by the Riverside".

Henrietta Lacks born Loretta Pleasant August 1, 1920- October 4, 1951 Lacks was a cervical cancer patient who while in treatment tissue sample were taken from her tumors without her or her family consent. In 1951 George Otto Gey culturated her cell into HeLa cells or HeLa immortal cell line a cell line which are still used in today's medical field. What made her cells so special is she had cell tread that stayed alive longer than a few hours to days which was not long enough to produce multiple test on unlike Lacks cells which could also be rapidly reproduced being the first cells to ever be successfully cloned in 1955. Her cells helped create the polio vaccine and helped with research for cancer, toxic substances, aids, radiation among other things. HeLa cells have almost eleven patents tied to it. Talk about a woman who helped society. Maryland declared August 1 Henrietta Lacks day in 2017.

Colin Powell born Colin Luther Powell on April 5, 1937 a man who has been awarded many military awards and decorations from both the United States and foreign countries as well. Highly recognized and respected man he received three electoral votes for POTUS in 2016. Colin served as the United States Secretary of State under George W Bush and was the first and only African American to serve as Joint Chiefs of Staff. Colin spends a lot of time now a days practicing public speaking.

Bayard Rustin born March 17, 1912- August 24, 1987 he was an activist for socialism, nonviolence, civil rights, gay rights and social movements. He was a leading activist who was a leader and influencer to some of the biggest activist including Martin Luther King Jr., Tom Kahn, and Stokely Carmichael. He even initiated a Freedom Ride in 1947.

Fannie Lou Hamer born Fannie Lou Townsend in Oct 6, 1917- March 14, 1977 coining the phrase Mississippi appendectomy involuntary or uninformed sterilization of black woman a common practice that took place in the south in the 1960s received a hysterectomy without her consent.

Zelda Wynn Valdes born June 28 1905- September 26 2001 fashion designer said to be the original designer for the Playboy Bunny costume.

Mary fields born 1832-1914 also known as Stagecoach

Mary and Black Mary was a cook, domestic worker, and freighter above all else the first African American woman star route mail carrier. Therefore she was a self-employed business woman.

Ruby bridges born Ruby Nell Bridges Hall September 8 1954 is the first African American child to desegregate the then all white school William-Frantz Elementary School being the only black child in the whole school in Louisiana in 1960. If it weren't for one teacher Barbara Henry Bridges may have not learned. One teacher taught Bridges as if she were teaching a whole class.

Sarah rector born March 3, 1902- July 22, 1967 Sarah was born on Indian Territory to parents who were descendants of slaves to Indians who were listed as freedmen on the Dawes Rolls who were allotted land under the Treaty of 1866 made by the United States with the Five Civilized Tribes. The land allotted to Rector was considered infertile soil not suitable for farming. The land began to be burden and Rector Father tried to sell but because of the land being called inferior and infertile they could not sell. In 1911 Rectors father leased her land to the Standard Oil Company in 1913 an independent oil driller drilled a well on the property with produced 2,500 barrels of oil a day bringing Rector 300 dollars a day, multiple wells were produced on site and rectos property subsequently became part of CUSHING-Drumright Oil Field. If you continue your research you will see how some thought this wealthy twelve year old was a young white girl verse the first self-made African American child.

George Washington Carver born 1860s- January 5, 1943 was an inventor and plant scientist. Carver's thing was peanuts he found them to be useful in a million ways, he also experimented with sweet potatoes and soybeans. He wanted to help people by urging them to alternate their cotton field with these practices. It resulted in improved cotton yields and also alternative cash crops. Carver also taught at the Tuskegee Institute as the head of the Agriculture Department for over 40 years. If you continue your research you'll teach this a man that wasn't even believed to live over twenty five.

Jackie Robinson born Jack Roosevelt "Jackie" Robinson January 31, 1919- October 24, 1972 was the first African American to play in Major League Baseball as a baseball second baseman. He signed to Brooklyn Dodgers in April 15 1947 after racial segregation. In 1997 his number 42 was retired being the first pro athlete in any sport to do so. April 15 is "Jackie Robinson Day" where every player on every team wears number 42. This was adopted an annual tradition on April 2004. Read up on him to learn his many awards, his first at UCLA for himself and his school, military days and more. His very successful breakthrough with baseball encouraged steady integration in Baseball with tennis and basketball following suit.

Rosa Parks born Rosa Louise McCauley Parks February 4,1913- October 24, 2005 Parks was also known as "the mother of the civil rights freedom movement" and "the first lady of civil rights" Parks is best known for not giving up her seat in the colored section of the bus so a white rider could sit. Even though she was not the first or only person to refuse parting with her seat NAACP probably because of her ties with them as a secretary thought she would the best face/candidate for moving forward with a court challenge. She was arrested for civil disobedience for violating segregation laws on December 1 1955. Research more of learn her involvement in the NAACP, Black Power movement, and political Prisoners.

Sojourner Truth born Isabella "Bell" Baumfree 1797- November 26, 1883 Truth was a human rights activist, abolitionist, and author. Truth was a very powerful woman who was very religious. Truth was born into slavery later becoming a runaway with her infant daughter and first African American woman to win a case of gaining custody of her son against a white man.

Claudette Colvin born September 5, 1939 was the first person to refuse to give up her seat on March 2, 1955 which led to her arrest at the age of fifteen. Colvin was one of the original plaintiffs in the Browder v. Gayle trial. Colvin was an active member in the NAACP Youth Council. She was then described as a hot head, out spoken, and mouthy. Go do some research on her definitely doesn't hold her tongue no wonder she helped make a difference. On March 2 1955 Claudette Colvin 15yr old would not give her seat up two months before Rosa parks.

Bessie Coleman born January 26, 1892- April 30, 1926.

Being a women and African American she had to save all her money to move to France to become a licensed pilot. She became the first African American women civil aviator, and became a successful air show pilot in the United States. In 1926 she died in a plane crash testing her new aircraft stopping her from fulfilling her goal to start a pilot school for African Americans.

Hiram Rhodes Revels born September 27, 1827- January 16, 1901 Revels was a college administer, minister and Republican politician. The first black senator Hiram Revels in 1870 officially joined U.S. Congress in Mississippi.

Dr. Sebi born Alfredo Darrington Bowman November 26, 1933- August 6, 2016 Dr. Sebi was a healer, biochemist, herbalist, pathologist and naturalist. He believed an Alkaline diet staying away from process foods, fructose, some dairy, meat, genetic modified organisms, foods that contribute to disease mucus being the main thing witch he believe caused sickness in the body. He was well known around the celebrity community also. The reason behind his arrested in Honduras is for having too much cash 37000 to be exact they later claimed he died of pneumonia after two days of being in jail. He started a 200 million dollar project known to cure sickle cell HIV/AIDS diabetes arthritis stroke and cancer. Go check out his approved foods and recipes know to reverse disease and strengthen a weak body.

Nat king Cole born Nathaniel Adams Coles March 17 1919- February 15, 1965 was singer Cole was one the first African Americans to host national television. Do some research on him learn his struggles in the music industry as well as with racism and a bit of back lash from the NAACP. Good man strong man…UNFORGETTABLE.

Ernie Davis born Ernest Davis December 14, 1939- May 18 1963 was the first African American football player (halfback) to win the Heisman Trophy in 1961 making him you guessed it a first pick in the 1962 NFL Draft. Although he seen his dreams come into fruition he never actually plucked them because of his leukemia. Learn more about his story there is even a movie based off his life "The Express".

Ann Lowe born Ann Cole Lowe 1898- February 25, 1981 first African American to become a highly noted fashion designer.

Lemuel Hayes known as the first black minister ordained in the congregational nomination of 1785. He ministered in all white churches in four different states. In 1804 he became the first African American to earn a master degree; he earned it from Middlebury College. Every year for George Washington birthday he preached a special sermon for about him.

Madame C.J. Walker born Sarah Breedlove December

23, 1867- May 25, 1919 was political social activist, philanthropist, and entrepreneur. What she is most known for is her hair and beauty products she had with African American women in mind. Walker is pegged the first female self-made millionaire in America, the most successful female entrepreneur of her time.

Maya Angelou was born Marguerite Annie Johnson born April 4 1928-May 28 2014 Maya Angelou was a renowned American poet, and civil activist. She published several books of essays, poetry and autobiographies. Her most popular work is "I Know Why the Caged Bird Sings" produced in 1969. She was the second poet to make an inaugural recitation in 1993 reciting her poem "On the Pulse of the Morning". If you research her you'll find she lived a very interesting life that she was very open about with no remorse. Maya Angelou had one child which also made her life interesting because of her son's baby mother, if I got into depth about this woman it would be one fourth of this book.

Booker T. Washington born Booker Taliaferro Washington April 5, 1856- November 14, 1915 one of the last generation of African American leaders born into slavery one of the most influential leaders of his time. Built an institution becoming one the leading powerful educators and power brokers.

Assata Shakur born JoAnne Deborah Byron on July 16, 1947 is an Activist. If I could interview anyone to create an action packed movie she would definitely be it! Go ahead research find out for yourself.

Tupac Amaru Shakur born Lesane Parish Crooks June 16, 1971- September 13, 1996 he was also known by his stage names 2Pac or Makaveli he was a song writer, producer, rapper, activist, actor, and poet. Check out his book "The Rose That Grew from Concrete" he reached all races and ages through his music alone. A decade after his death he finally had a movie put about him mid-year 2017.

Dick Gregory Born Richard Claxton "Dick" Gregory October 12, 1932 – August 19,2017 he is a civil rights activist, writer, entrepreneur, Author, comedian, critic. Advocate and believer of Organ Harvesting and Planned Parenthood being Black Genocide research him he gives his point of view in refreshing direct funny manner.

Marcus Garvey born Marcus Mosiah Garvey Jr. born August 17, 1887-june 10, 1940 born a Jamaican and first awarded by the ONH Jamaica (Order of National Hero). Garvey was a political leader, entrepreneur, founder, journalist, publisher, and public speaker. He founded the Universal Negro Improvement Association and African Communities league and the Black star line. His publishing of Negro World was his voice a weekly newspaper that lived from 1918-1933. Garvey has an influence that is major The UNIA red black and green colors has been adopted as the Black Liberian Flag. Dr. Martin Luther King recognized him by saying "He was the first man of color to lead and develop a mass movement. He was the first man on a mass scale and level to give millions of Negros a sense of dignity and destiny. And make a Negro feel he was somebody."

King Mansa Musu (emperor) 1312-1337 Mali Empire worth 400 billion. He had so much gold he was just giving it away. LOL. Interesting man.

Anthony Johnson born 1600-1670 he was indentured servant/slave. After his contract was up he became one of the first African American property owner and slave owner. He became a very successful tobacco farmer. He is recognized for accumulating large wealth after serving his term of indenture. You may have heard someone refer to him as "the black patriarch".

Elijah Muhammad born Elijah Robert Poole October 7, 1897-Februaruy 25, 1975 Muhammad was the leader of NOI before Farrakhan. He was a mentor to Malcolm X and Muhammad Ali.

Louis Farrakhan born Louis Eugene Wolcott May 11, 1933 Farrakhan is a religious leader, activist, and social commentator. He is best known for his role as the leader of the Nation of Islam. This man doesn't look his age.

Adam Kirby this little guy is the youngest member of Mensa he was invited at the age of 2yr and four months and then gained full access membership at the age of two years and five months he scored 141 on the Stanford-Binet IQ test *This is definitely worth putting in the notables lol*

Biddy Mason born Bridget "Biddy" Mason August 15 1818- January 15, 1891 was a nurse, philanthropist, and real estate. She is the founder of the first African Methodist Episcopal Church. She was born a slave but became a free woman one of the first to buy land in California. She spoke Spanish and was well know name in the community loved so much some called her "Grandma Mason" or "Auntie Mason"

Oprah Winfrey born Orpah Gail Winfrey January 29, 1954 is a talk show host, producer, actress, philanthropist, and media proprietor. Some call her the "Queen of All Media" and "Most influential woman in the world" Oprah is to date North Americas first and only multi-billionaire Black person. She probably doesn't ever answer her phone, but seriously look up Oprah she has definitely been and overcome a lot while maintaining a heart, no wonder she's loved nationwide.

Martin Delany born Martin Robinson Delany May 6, 1812- January 24, 1885 was a journalist, writer, abolitionist, and physician. He was one of the first three black people admitted into Harvard Medical School. Some call Delany the grandfather of Black Nationalism.

Nina Simone born Eunice Kathleen Waymon February

21, 1933- April 21 2003 was singer, songwriter, civil rights activist, pianist, and music arranger.

Nelson Mandela first black president of South Africa May 10 1994 to June 14 1999 born July 18 1918 died Dec. 5 2013 at the age of 95 he had six kids married three times. Nick names were Madiba meaning father of a nation and Dalibunga meaning "founder of the Bunga" Bunga means new. He was an activist politician philanthropist and lawyer. He was most known for his Anti-Apartheid Movement and book 'Long Walk to Freedom" a winner of over 200 honors and a winner of Nobel peace prize also became a subject of cult personality labeled someone with charismatic authority. June 12 1964 sentence to life in prison release Feb. 1990.

W.E.B. Du Bois born William Edward Burghardt "WEB" Du Bois February 23, 1868- August 27, 1963 age of 95 *I'm sure he witnessed a lot and was so close to seeing the goal reached.* Du Bois was as a sociologist, historian, civil rights activist, pan Africanist. Co-founder of NAACP IN 1909 the founder in the Niagara Movement. Du Bois's main focus was racism he would strongly protest discrimination due to work and education, lynching and Jim Crow laws. His main support was Africans and Asians. He is wildly known for his writings over 30 publishing's. He believed blacks needed a strong classical education in order to reach their full potential. Web du Bois died a day before MLK famous speech.

There are probably a couple saying well what about

"him" and "her" just hold your horses this is just the beginning a lot of people and different events will be mentioned in this little book. I just want to stop and say these few mentioned nine out of ten were raised in a tough era very hateful and tiring and they all stood for something real and relevant. Not saying that today's times are a piece of cake the point is they believed and fought knowing tiny and huge consequences a time when anything had a huge consequence. Just know one thing about them all they were or very much still today all very black and proud thinking and believing above all the prejudice and stereotypes that were ultimately set against us.

> *"The progress of the world will call for the best that all of us have to give."*
>
> *Mary McLeod Bethune*

MELANIN

Netta B.

NOTES

MELANIN

THIS IS JUST A TEST TO SEE WHAT YOU KNOW

98% of the multiple choice answers is a person, topic, and date that is worth researching.

He was a patented inventor and historian film writer.

- A. Redd Foxx
- B. Henry T. Sampson
- C. Jesse Eugene Russell
- D. Bernie Mack

She is the first and only black woman to debut at number one on the Billboard hot 100 and named one of the top 3 best female artist of the United States by RIAA.

- E. Lauryn Hill
- F. Billie Holiday
- G. Mariah Carey
- H. Solange

Angela Bassett played the Tina Turner's character in the "What's Love Got to Do with It".

a. True
b. False

In 2009 Disney made their 49th Disney animated feature and First African American Disney Princess in "The Princess and the Frog" staring voice of _____ as Tiana.

A. Regina king
B. Brenda Skyes
C. Anika Noni Rose
D. Monica

Who was the first Kenyan and Mexican actress to win an academy award?

A. Nini Wacera
B. Patricia Kihoro
C. Lupita Nyong'o
D. Janet Mbugua

What are some things Haile Selassie born Tafari Makonnen Woldemikael on July 23 1892- august 27 1892 Emperor of Ethiopia accomplish?

A. Help found the Rastafari Movement
B. Abolished all legal basis of slavery and slave trading in his empire on August 27, 1942
C. A, B, D
D. Ethiopia's first written Constitution

Michael B Jordan played the lead role of Oscar Grant in the movie "Fruitvale Station".

A. True
B. False

Whose trail was significate in the south mainly the state of FL Back in the year 1959?

A. Recy Taylor
B. Joan Little
C. Betty Jean Owens
D. Jo Ann Robinson

Who was the first dark skinned woman to cross over into mainstream advertising/modeling in 1950? Starting off as a stylist at the age of 17 she was founded and began an exclusive modeling with Jet and Ebony magazine. She also worked modeling/brand ambassador for Budweiser, Christian Dior and Sears.

A. Naomi Sims
B. Beverly Johnson
C. Helen Williams
D. Alek Wek

Laurence C Jones born Laurence Clifton Jones November 21 1882-July 13-1975 founder of _____ the second oldest continually operating African American boarding school?

　A. Spellman College
　B. Providence St Mel
　C. Piney Woods Country Life School
　D. Dunbar High School

His mother was shot in church multiple times while playing the Piano on a Sunday morning?

　A. Malcolm X
　B. Muhammad Ali
　C. Martin Luther King
　D. Sam Cooke

Alice Marie Coachman was the first Black woman to win Olympic Gold in _____ London Olympic Games for high jump?

　A. 1938
　B. 1967
　C. 1948
　D. 1957

What is Sammy Davis known for saying?

　A. "Music is life"
　B. "Why does the cage bird sing"
　C. "Talk about handicap, I'm a one-eyed Negro Jew."
　D. All the above

Jack Wiggins was a tap dancer known for tango twist he also tapped danced and told jokes.

A. True
B. False

Referred to as the poet laureate of television, he played the tin man on the Wiz. He was the first black performer to become a regular panelist on a daily network game show in 1964.

A. Ted Ross
B. Willie C. Carpenter
C. Nipsey Russell
D. Michael Jackson

Wallace Thurman created:

A. OZONE Magazine in 2002
B. JET Magazine in 1951
C. Outlet Magazine in early 1920's
D. The Crisis Magazine in 1910

Aaron Douglas was considered the _____.

A. "Father of Soul"
B. "Father of words"
C. "Father of African American Art"
D. "Father of the people"

He was the first man to set three world records in one Olympic game.

A. Scotty Pippen
B. Roy Jones JR.
C. Usain Bolt
D. Carl Lewis

_____ helped negotiate the capture of Robert Gram.

A. Barack Obama
B. Rev. Al Sharpton
C. Jessie Jackson
D. Colin Powell

Kwame Nkrumah

A. Led Ghana to independence
B. Served as Ghana president
C. A, B, and D
D. Served as Ghana first prime minister

_____ holds several Guinness World Records highest annual earning pop star best-selling album of all time most Grammys in a year.

A. James Brown
B. Miles Davis

C. Michael Jackson
D. Otis Mayfield

William Powell built his own _____ in 1960 using his own land and taught neighborhood kids to play, it all started because he wasn't allowed to play on the white only course he died in 2010 at the age of 93.

A. Amusement park
B. Bumper cars
C. Golf course
D. Track

Singer Tammi Terrell (Thomasina Winifred Montgomery, I liked her name) died at 25 of a _____.

A. Heart attack
B. Coma
C. Brain tumor
D. Cancer

Whose child was said to conspire to kill Louise Farrakhan and died three weeks after their grandchild set fire to their home?

A. Coretta Scott King
B. Angela Davis
C. Betty Shabazz
D. Assata Shakur

Quvenzhan'e Wallis is youngest actress ever nominated for Academy Award for Best Actress and the first born in the twenty first century to be nominated for an Oscar.

A. False
B. True

Who was the woman ever to serve on staff at Jules Stein Eye Institute? No woman ever headed over a post-grad training program in ophthalmology, or been elected to the honorary staff of the UCLA Medical Center and the first Black woman to serve on staff as a surgeon at the UCLA Medical Center.

A. Raven Symone
B. Lauryn hill
C. Patricia Bath
D. Dinah Shore

_____born November 19, 1960 – present was the first drag queen supermodel?

A. Andrea Jenkins
B. Grace Jones
C. RuPaul
D. BeBE Zahara Benet

_____ born Ruth Lee Jones was the "Queen of Blues" the most popular black female artist of the 50s.

A. Cicely Tyson

B. Aretha Franklin
C. Dinah Washington
D. Billie Holiday

She was a singer dancer actress in 1970 one of history highest paid Las Vegas performer the queen of Vegas 100,000 a week to perform, first African American to model for a cosmetic line not solely targeted for blacks.

A. Mary White Ovington
B. Debbie Allen
C. Lola Falana
D. Niecy Nash

Black lives matter was founded by Alicia Garza, Opal Tometi, and Portisse Cullors after George Zimmerman was acquitted for killing an unarmed teenager Trayvon Martin on July 13, 2013 but officially recognized following the deaths of Eric Garner and Michael Brown.

A. False
B. True

What show rated as the number one show in America for five years airing from 1984-1992?

A. Good Times
B. The Jefferson's
C. The Cosby Show
D. A Different World

She was the first African woman to integrate a beauty contest in America, first African American Miss Subways.

A. Tyra Banks
B. Vanessa Williams
C. Thelma Porter
D. Iman

Macon Allen born Macon Boiling Allen August 4, 1816 – June 11 1894 passed the bar exam in 1844 became justice of peace in mass in 1848 a probate court judge in 1874 in south Carolina.

A. Believed to be the first African American to graduate and study science in the U.S.
B. Was the first African American to graduate and be licensed to practice medicine in the U.S.
C. Believed to be the first African American to graduate and be licensed to practice law in the U.S.
D. Was the only African American to graduate and be licensed to practice law in the U.S.

Who wrote the novel "Their Eyes Were Watching God?"

A. Terry McMillan
B. Sista Soulja
C. Zora Neale Hurston
D. Mya Angelou

Who wrote a book with a collection of African American writings that became a land mark in Black literature known as the "first national book" of African Americans (the New Negro)?

   A. Spike Lee
   B. Frederick Douglas
   C. Alain Locke
   D. James Weldon Johnson

Believed to be the first African American to file and win a lawsuit in the United States Called "the first really successful colored lawyer in America".

   A. Tommy Biggs
   B. John Cochran
   C. Robert Morris
   D. Thomas Jones

Who said "I was a victim of stereo type. There was only two of us negro kids in the whole class and our English teacher was always stressing the importance of rhythm in poetry. Well, everyone knows, except us, that all Negros have rhythm, so they elected me as class poet."

   A. John Singleton
   B. George Tillman Jr
   C. Langston Hughes
   D. John Peele

Who smuggled military intelligence to French allies during WWII pinning secrets inside her dress and hiding them in her sheet music?

- A. Tammi Terrell
- B. Diana Ross
- C. Josephine Baker
- D. Dorothy Dandridge

"The Ethel Waters Show" aired on June 14, 1939 was the first African American to star in her own show via television, it being a special variety show.

- A. False
- B. True

She survived three assignation attempts while running for the 1971 Democratic nomination to U.S. presidency.

- A. Elaine Brown
- B. Dr. Lee Thornton
- C. Shirley Chrisholm
- D. Maxine Waters

Johnnie Cochran born Johnnie L. Cochran Jr. on October 2, 1937- March 29, 2005 the defense lawyer was what some may call a celebrity lawyer. What are three case profiles below he is known for.

- A. Rae Carruth, Sandra Bland, and Tamir Rice
- B. John Allen Muhammad, Freddie Gray, and Walter

Scott
C. Michael Jackson, O.J. Simpson, and Sean Combs
D. Michael Brown, Eric Garner, and Rodney King

Harlem Globetrotters consist of athleticism, exhibition basketball, theater, and _____.

A. Dance
B. Soccer
C. Comedy
D. Studying

Who is said to be the first African American woman to complete a four year course of college of university completing a ladies literary course at Oberlin College in 1850?

A. Sarah Jane Woodson Early
B. Lucy Ann Stanton
C. Mary Jane Patterson
D. Sojourner truth

Who owns Solar Energy Electricity in Africa founded in 2014 providing electricity for over fourteen countries?

A. Djimon Hounsou, Africa
B. Iman, Africa
C. Akon, Africa
D. Thandie Newton, Africa

Who stole a transport ship dressed as the captain uses the confederates own hand signals and codes helping others slaves and families and escape to freedom while later in life ran for politician and won?

A. David Alexander Paterson
B. Colin Powell
C. Robert Smalls
D. Roland Wallace Burris

He was the first black news anchor in the United States first television journalist to die of AIDS he was the founder of the National Association of Black Journalist.

A. Bernard Shaw
B. Randall Robinson
C. Max Robinson
D. Magic Johnson

Harry Belafonte the _____ was the first African American to win an Emmy.

A. "King of Rock"
B. "King of Dance"
C. "King of Calypso"
D. "King of acting"

Bill Cosby was the creator of "Fat Albert and the Cosby Kids" the cartoon aired 1972-1985 being one of the longest running Saturday Morning cartoons.

A. True
B. False

Sydney Poitier was first African American to win Academy Award for best actor in _____ 1963.

A. "Let's Do It Again"
B. "Guess Who's Coming To Dinner"
C. "Lilies of the Field"
D. "13TH"

_____ based off of The Wonderful Wizard of Oz stared an all-black cast and marked the end to the Blaxploitation movement era in 1978.

A. Beast of no Nation
B. ROOTS
C. The Wiz
D. Uptown Saturday Night

Who is the first African American to receive an Oscar?

A. Samuel L. Jackson
B. James Basket
C. Sidney Poitier
D. John Kitzmiller

James brown "Godfather of Soul" rolling stone most sampled artist of all time Wrote _____ in 1960 giving all the royalties to _____.

- A. "This is a Man's World", women's rights program
- B. "Rolling Stone", homeless youth program
- C. "Don't be a Drop Out", drop-out prevention program
- D. "Love", all the lovers

The "Prince of Soul" father shot him in the heart and shoulder while he was sleeping. He was killed after getting slightly physical and breaking up a fight between his parents.

- A. William Grant Still
- B. Marvin Gaye
- C. Al Green
- D. Count Basie

_____ is the first African American to play Cinderella on Broadway.

- A. Juanita Hall
- B. Brandy
- C. Keke Palmer
- D. Matilda Sissieretta Joyner Jones

She was the "Empress of Blues"

- A. Millie Jackson
- B. Bessie Smith

C. Bessie Coleman
D. Ma Rainey

Her main protest was against lynching she felt it was a major problem because it was unjust mainly used on people of color. Lynching increased as price of cotton declined and it was a form of community control. She was known as an anti-lynching crusader.

A. Ruby Dee
B. Mary McLeod Bethune
C. Ida B. Wells
D. Jane Matilda Bolin

She was the first African American to be nominated for an Academy Award in the best actress category, first African American female to be on the cover of Life Magazine.

A. Maggie L. Walker
B. Mary Eliza Mahoney
C. Dorothy Jean Dandridge
D. Rebecca Davis Lee Crumpler

Flint water crisis in 2014 health issues began when flint changed its source of drinking water leaving the Detroit River and Lake Huron and replacing the water source to the Flint River without changing its pipes or applying corrosion inhibitors leading the residents to exposure of lead poisoning and the possible outbreak of Legionnaires disease. After the reassignment, firing, lawsuits, federal state of emergency, and apology from the Governor in 2017 the water is now considered acceptable but complete pipe replacement expected by 2020.

   A. True
   B. False

Who is "FloJo" she is considered the fastest woman in the world.

   A. Simone Biles
   B. Dominique Dawes
   C. Jackie Joyner
   D. Sheryl Swoops

He opened his home as Underground Railroad depot and opened a school for black children.

   A. James Wormley Jones
   B. William Cooper Nell
   C. James Forten
   D. Captain Michael Healy

She is the first black woman to make it onto Broadway "A Raisin in the Sun".

   A. Phyllis Hyman
   B. Carmen Jones
   C. Lorriane Hansberry
   D. Mildred Washington

Mama Janet Ekundayo is considered _____.

- A. "Goddess of Africa"
- B. "Face of Africa"
- C. "Mother Theresa of Africa"
- D. "Love of Africa"

She is the first African American woman to play Belle of Beauty and the Beast on Broadway.

- A. Amanda Randolph
- B. Aaliyah
- C. Toni Braxton
- D. Micki Grant

Who gets dibs on the term "The real McCoy"?

- A. Mildred McCoy
- B. George McCoy
- C. Elijah McCoy
- D. Macoy McCoy

Her "HeLa" cells help cure Polio. First human cells grown in a lab that could be described as immortal cells doctors profited off her cells without her or her family permission and knowledge.

- A. Sherian Cadoria
- B. Wilma Rudolph
- C. Henrietta Lacks

D. Karen Batchelor

Will Smith and DJ Jazzy Jeff won the first rap Grammy in February 22, 1989 for the single _____.

   A. "Summatime"
   B. "Ring My Bell"
   C. "Parents Just Don't Understand"
   D. "Yo Home to Bel Air"

Known as the first Black Television sitcom show to air on television was "Julia" in 1968 followed by "Sanford and Son" in 1972.

   A. True
   B. False

Who owns Boss Life Construction, affordable housing company out of Texas?

   A. Beyoncé
   B. Pimp C
   C. Slim Thug
   D. Kelly Rowland

Did some Africans really keep slave raiders away by training killer bees to keep them from their territories AND by living on water in houses built on stilts?

   A. True

B. False

Henrietta Lacks isn't the only person to have something done without her knowledge. Fannie Lou Hamer while removing a tumor a doctor preformed a hysterectomy without her knowledge coining the phase "Mississippi Appendectomy".

A. True
B. False

Gloria Richardson leader of The Cambridge Movement during the Civil Rights Movement.

A. True
B. False

Althea Gibson Tennis and golf player first African American to win a Grand Slam title.

A. True
B. False

The black cabinet, Federal Council of Negro Affairs and the Black Brain Trust are all the same thing.

A. True
B. False

_____ was a best-selling novel of the 19th century and second best book following the Bible.

   A. Poems on Various Subjects, Religious and Moral
   B. The Reaper
   C. Uncle Tom's Cabin
   D. The Brownies Book

Shaka Zulu own brothers attempted to kill him twice before success.

   A. True
   B. False

Abraham Lincoln was good friends/acquaintances with Frederick Douglas. Some think he died for this very reason wanting to help Douglas's race.

   A. True
   B. False

Bill Richman was a born slave who turned internationally known boxer known as "The Black Terror" and having a white wife.

   A. True
   B. False

First black woman to win an Academy Award for Best Actress March 24 2002.

   A. Jennifer Jackson
   B. Ann Lowe
   C. Halle Berry
   D. Camilla Williams

First African American to win skating world champion in 1986

   A. Misty Copeland
   B. Sheila Johnson
   C. Debi Thomas
   D. Alice Coachman

Whoopi Goldberg first African American to win all Emmy Grammy Oscar and Tony second to win an Academy award.

   A. True
   B. False

Tennis stars known as "Pete and Repeat".

   A. Serena and Venus Williams
   B. Evelyn Ashford
   C. Margaret and Matilda Peters
   D. Ibtihaj Muhammad

Fannie Lou Hamer born Fannie Lou Townsend in Oct 6, 1917- March 14, 1977 coining the phrase Mississippi appendectomy involuntary or uninformed sterilization of black woman a common practice that took place in the south in the 1960s received a hysterectomy without her consent.

    A. True
    B. False

First black model to appear on the cover of Vogue magazine.

    A. Gail Fisher
    B. Vanessa L Williams
    C. Donyale Luna
    D. Niaomi Campbell

"Priestess of Soul" she hated the name.

    A. Grace Bumbry
    B. Leontyne Price
    C. Nina Simone
    D. Ella Fitzgerald

This activist wasn't scared of titles; she was a self-described black lesbian mother warrior poet.

    A. Charlene Mitchell

B. Ava Du Vernay
C. Audre Lorde
D. Dina Flecher

Usain bolt holds both one hundred and two hundred meters relay world record.

A. True
B. False

William Fletcher Penn born January 16, 1871- May 31, 1934 first African American to graduate from Yale Medical College and staff on their yearbook. Louis Wright was his step-father.

A. True
B. False

He was a four time gold medalist in the 1936 Olympic Games.

A. Wilt Chamberlain
B. Kareem Abdul-Jabbar
C. Jessie Owens
D. Jim Brown

Finished school and college together in same week at age 16, criminal justice is her family niche.

A. Patricia Roberts Harris
B. Carol Moseley Braun
C. Grace Bush
D. Ola Hudson

Lena Horne born Lena Mary Calhoun Horne June 30 1917- May 9 2010. Horne was dancer, actress, civil rights activist, and jazz and pop music singer.

A. True
B. False

She was the first African American women to start her own route mail carrier in the U.S.

A. Elizabeth Keckley
B. Lenora Fulani
C. Mary Fields
D. Azie Taylor Morton

She is said to be the brains behind the infamous Playboy Bunny costume.

A. Carly Cushnie
B. Kimora Lee Simmons
C. Zelda Wynn Valdes
D. Ann Lowe

He was the first African American in space.

A. Joseph L. Searles III
B. Daniel James Jr.
C. Guion Stewart Bluford Jr.
D. Donnie Cochran

Martin Luther King Jr. was killed on Maya Angelo birthday April 4 1968. She stopped celebrating for a while but annually sent flowers to Mrs. King until her death.

A. True
B. False

Web du Bois died a day before Martin Luther King Jr. famous speech.

A. True
B. False

The first book published by a black woman.

A. The Heroic Slave
B. The Uncalled
C. Poems on Various Subjects, Religious and Moral
D. Clotel: or, The Presidents Daughter

Strange fruit by Billie Holiday was a poem written by

Abel Meerpol a Jewish school teacher.

   A. True
   B. False

"No One is immune to the trials and tribulations of life"

Martin Lawrence

Netta B.

MELANIN

NOTES

Netta B.

INVENTORS/INVENTIONS

This is one of my favorites! I mean when I tell you we are some smart individuals so innovative, it blows my mind. The list below is also just a few more people in my eyes that helped build this thing called "Civilized Living" Naw I'm just kidding or am I? LOL. A lot of the below inventions came during a time when a few of the inventors were still slaves or previously a slave a mentally draining point at time in their life I'm sure. Yet they still completed and proved whatever point or theory they were working on. Majority of these inventions were and are a betterment in our now society.

In this chapter you will see just how much your race contributed to this society. In my eyes if there are so many people of color inventions that are still very relevant in today's times, how and why is this a white man's land? Which further leads me to how people can assume POC are so lazy, stupid, criminals, and or a waste of breath? I believe every race and gender can be all of the above so to just label a specific race is unjust. What it is, is a mind thing we see it we hear it so everyone believes it. *Especially us.*

All leading to every ones individuality you are smart, you have ideas, but you go back to the media or "friends" and now you feel you're stupid; it won't work, or not cool enough. If you do this or that what will "They" say? Nothing! Don't tell "They" handle your business and share when it's over and done with. You cannot worry about your friends or the opinion of others they don't dictate your life you do. A true friend is going to do nothing more than encourage you celebrate you and have a thorough reason of why it's a grand or not so good plan. If they do nothing that I have stated then that is not your friend but a wolf in sheep's attire and you need to distance yourself immediately. Be like somebody below who just focused.

I couldn't name them all but you will get the just of it.

Thomas L Jennings: Patented a dry cleaning process that was known to be the first African American Patent in 1821.

John H. Allen

Dr. Shirley Ann Jackson: (August 5, 1946- present) is the brain child for the breakthrough research and technology that helped others to create the touch tone phone, fiber optic cables, solar cells, the tech behind caller ID and call waiting, and the portable fax.

Rene Lacoste: (July 2, 1904- October 12, 1996) created Lacoste Brand a champion tennis player who founded his logo based off a lost bet. "He didn't win his crocodile case but he sure did fight like a crocodile" in 1929 Lacoste tennis shirt/brand was born. Most claim Lacoste to be white but his mother was Jamaican and his father French.

Maurice W. Lee Sr.: pressure cooker

Jerry Lawson: born Gerald Anderson "Jerry" Lawson December 1, 1940-April 9, 2011 an computer engineer. In my mind the reason men play so many games…should have known a man can up with the idea of game console.

David Harper: Book Case (heart eyes to this guy lol)

M.C. Harney: replaced candles with the invention of the lantern lamp. Patent Aug, 19, 1884.

Madame C.J. walker: created hair care and skin care products to her black consumers. There are two stories to how she came up with her products. One is a man came to her in a dream telling her what ingredients to use and she did. *I wish some lottery numbers would come to me in my dreams* The second is after stress called her to lose hair she searched for an answer to reverse the curse in the late 1800's she found her recipe and began to grow and market in the early 1900's leaving her to be one of the first self-made millionaire. What's your illness or weakness can you self-heal and pass it on and make profit.

Leonard C. Bailey

Marie Van Brittan Brown: (October 30, 1922- February 2, 1999) invented home security system in 1966 patented on Dec. 2, 1969.

Eunice W. Johnson: (April 4, 1916- January 3, 2010) creator of Ebony Fashion Fair in 1950's wife of John H. Johns Fashion fair one of the first black owned beauty companies. She seen how models had to mix foundations and created Fashion Fair.

Virgie M. Ammons

Frederick McKinley Jones: (may 17, 1893- February 21, 1961) created air conditioning unit, refrigerated truck which became a 3 million dollar company and very important during the world war 2 to carry perishables medicine and blood. Jones also invented a device to combine sound with motion picture. In total Jones had 61 patents he co-founded Thermo King.

Matthew A. Cherry: street car fender patent on Jan. 1, 1895 tricycle patent on May 8, 1888.

Lester A. Lee

Kenneth J. Dunkley: invented 3D glasses.

George Crum: born George Speck 1824-July 22, 1914. An Indian or mulatto chef who created the potato chip in the 1850's.

Dr. Jane C. Wright: born Jane Cooke Wright November 30, 1919- February 19, 2013) also known as Jane Jones. Jones was a surgeon and cancer researcher she tested human sells instead of animal tissue, and created a sequence and pattern to make chemo more effective. Wright's father **Louis Tompkins Wright** July 23, 1891- October 8, 1952, was a civil activist and surgeon who was the first African American surgeon of a non-segregated hospital first prominent doctor in Atlanta, and first African American to own a vehicle in the city. Both made a big contribution for and to chemotherapy.

Jesse Eugene Russell: with around 100 patents Russell holds seven patents which make him a key player in the cell phone invention.

Samuel R. Scottron: extendable Curtin rod.

Albert C. Richardson: casket lowering and the butter churn.

Alexander P. Ashbourne

Paul Eugene Belcher and Daniel Hobel: in 1982 made remote AC power control.

Phillip B. Downing: patented the letter box better known as the mail box, Downing designed a metal letter box with four legs on October 27 1891.

Dr. Walter McAfee: born Walter S. McAfee (September 2, 1914- February 18, 1990) astronomer and scientist. Known for his participation with Project Diana, the world's first lunar radar echo experiments.

Dr. Hadiyah-Nicole Green: laser cancer treatment while avoiding healthy cells and with little to no side effects Green is also one of the 66 black women to earn a Ph. D in physics in the United States between 1973 AND 2012.

Robert Pelham: patented the tallying device in 1913 and the tabulation device in 1905.

Isaac R. Johnson

Bessie Blount Griffin invented the kidney dish or a emesis which was disposable a disposable version and in 1951 she invented a electric feeding device for amputee's when after biting down on the tube it would deliver a mouth-full of food neither invention were accepted by The American Veterans Administration so the feeder she sold to the French and the basin she sold to Belgium.

The true inventor of **Jack Daniels** after 150 yrs. the truth the original recipe belonged to a black man named **Nearis Green or Nearest Green 1820-1890**. Green one of Dan Call slaves taught call how to distill. Call passed the recipe to Daniels. Over 150 yrs. Greens involvement was known to the local historians but only recently acknowledged by whiskey makers. It's said that Daniels opened a distillery hiring two of Greens sons. ***DYK**: K. Michelle is the 1st African American artist and person to have an endorsement deal with Jack Daniels*

W.A. Deitz: created a shoe patent in 1867 of an

improved designed women shoe to slip on and off.

William D. Davis: serving as a buffalo soldier he created and patented the horse saddle.

Marc B. Auguste

Bertha Berman: created fitted bed sheets in 1959

Sarah Boone: born Sarah Marshall 1832-1904 ironing board patent in April 26, 1892.

Lewis Latimer: improved Thomas Edison light bulb improving the longevity of the light leading him to become a big part of Edison's electrical Company in total Lewis held 8 U.S. Patents.

Oscar E. Brown: Horse shoe patent Aug, 23, 1892

Alexander Miles: born May 18, 1838- May 7 1918) invented a automatically opening and closing elevator door on October 11, 1887.

Alfred A Bishop

Otis Boykin: born Otis Bobby Boykin august 29, 1920- march 13, 1982) Boykin created the heart pacemaker he was an engineer known for twenty eight patents.

Garret Morgan: born Garrett Augustus Morgan March 4, 1877- July 27, 1963) he was also known as big chief mason. Morgan is known for a multitude of things he invented, he was a hero, and he was very active in the black community and organizations. Here are some inventions you may know him for... traffic light adding the third option slow down instead of just stop and go. The first smoke detection mask for fire fighters and he also invented the first hair straightening cram by pure accident. He was the first African American to own a vehicle in Cleveland Ohio.

Alice H. Parker: patented her design for the gas heating furnace on Dec. 23, 1919.

George W Carver: is known as the peanut butter man with over one hundred ways to use them but he never patent anything to claim that fame. His work helped with and one patent for cosmetics and two for paints and stains, he only patented three things out of three hundred worth of inventions. Carver had dozens of sweet potato, pecan, soybeans and peanut recipes and uses of these items for or as things like shampoo, shaving cream, lamp oil, gasoline, ink, laxatives, dyes really it's too much for me to name.

Humphrey H. Reynolds: safety gate on bridges

John S. Brooks

Alfred L. Cralle: ice cream scooper patent Feb. 2, 1897

Dr. Charles R. Drew: born Charles Richard Drew June 3, 1904-april 1, 1950) was a surgeon, medical researcher, and physician. He created the idea of blood banks, improved blood storage and preservation of blood plasma in the 1940's. Drew was the first African

American selected as an examiner on the American Board of Surgery. He fought that races could share blood as long as it was the same string or blood type this was his protest stop racial segregation even in blood. He soon resigned his position with American Red Cross. In 1950 the same year Drew died racial segregation in blood donation was no longer maintained.

Solomon Harper: electrical hair treating implement or thermostatic hair curlers in 1930.

Walter Sammons: on Feb. 19, 1924 patented an improved pressing comb, one with an insulated handle curved teeth and thermometer to check the temp.

William Harwell

Imhotep: known for the first use of stone columns to support buildings.

David M. Bondu: the golf tee in 1975

Anthony Brown: three patents for weather detectors

Dr. Betty Wright Harris: American chemist with patented invention to do spot test for identifying explosives in a field environment.

John Lee Love: 1897 invented the portable pencil sharpener

Daniel Hale Williams: born January 18, 1856 august 4, 1931 first African American to record a successful open heart surgery on July 9 1893. In 1891 Williams founded the Provident Hospital in Chicago Illinois, the first non-segregated hospital in the United States.

Harry C. Hopkins: enhancing the hearing aid.

Norman K Bucknor

John F. Pickering: air-ship patent on Feb. 20, 1900 or better known name the blimp.

William B. Purvis: is said to have invented a handful of things most patented a few not. Some of his patents are electric railway switch, hand stamp, bag fastener his most famous the fountain pen patented on Jan. 7, 1890. SN I would hate to have had to carry a bottle of ink in my bag, I'm too clumsy.

Lee S. Burridge & Marshman: improved type writer patent. (Newman R. Marshman)

George .T. Sampson: patent for mechanical clothes dryer 1892

Tanya R. Allen

Robert G Bryant: too many to name

FW Leslie: 1891 invented the envelope seal

Joseph Winters: fire escape ladder patent on May 6, 1882 which replaced the wood with metal frame and parallel steps. On May 7, 1878 he patented the wagon mounted fire escape ladder.

Alfred Benjamin: stainless steel scouring pads

Thomas J. Martin: made an improved patent on the fire extinguisher on March 26, 1872. I believe it to be more the inspiration for a fire hydrant and fire hose.

Granville T Woods: Born April 23, 1856- Jan. 30, 1910 owned around fifty patents was most known for his many improvements for a safer and smoother ride on trains and trolley car systems and his invention "telegraphony" allowing people to send telegraph and voice messages over a single wire. He was also the first black person to be a mechanical and electrical engineer he held over 50 patents including egg incubator and automatic brake, he was self-taught about the railroads and trains and street cars. His most accredited invention was a device that sent messages between moving trains and to train stations. Thomas Edison tried to claim two of his patents but failed. He offered woods a job but woods declined. He made improvement patents to telephone, telegraph, phonograph and more.

John Albert Burr: on May 9. 1899 made improvement patent to the lawn mower adding traction wheels and rotary blades. He holds other patents to improved lawn mower.

John Standard: made improvements the refrigerator and oil stove.

Francis Edward Butler

Charles Brooks: made improvements to both the truck sweeper and ticket hole puncher to where the ticket puncher collets the pieces instead of letting them fall.

George Edward Alcorn Jr.: holds eight patents influenced on the X-ray, Alcorn invented the X-ray Spectrometer created for scientist.

James Forten: born 1766 now even though he did not patent anything he invented a sail that was better for sailing at greater speeds and maneuvering his sail loft making him one of the most successful business the best thing about his story is more than half of his fortune was used towards abolitionist causes and buying slaves freedom.

Jack Johnson: patented the wrench on April 18, 1922. Johnson was also the first Black World Heavyweight Champion in 1908.

Turner Byrd Jr.

Richard Spikes: born Oct. 2, 1878- Jan. 22, 1963 held 12 patents but most known for his improvement to all vehicles from cars trucks to buses. He's the creator of the beer tap.

Thomas W. Steward: invented the mop connecting a stick to a cloth held by a metal clamp.

Lloyd Ray: patented the dust pan on Aug. 3, 1897 Dust

pan

Robert F, Flemming Jr.: on March 3. 1886 received patent for the "Euphonica" now called the guitar.

William h Richardson: improvement patent to the baby carriage/baby buggy June 18, 1889 making the carriage reversible so the pusher could face baby and fixing the axels on the wheels so it was more mobile and fit into smaller spaces.

Eugene Burkins: Machine gun

Benjamin Banneker: born November 9, 1731- October 9, 1806) created the Almanac in 1791 predicting seasonal and weather changes up to ten years before they happened and giving tip s of medical remedies and planting crops. At the age of 22 in 1753 created a wooden clock (that he hand carved) that struck on the hour creating the first clock ever built in the United States the clock read perfect time for thirty years all off the inspiration of a pocket watch. This man did all this being self-taught in reading and science.

Osbourn Dorsey: door stop Door knob 1878

Elijah McCoy: born Elijah J. McCoy May 2, 1844- October 10, 1929) McCoy had 57 US Patents most consuming of lubrication of steam engines. He also produced a folding ironing board, and water lawn sprinkler.

Lonnie Johnson: born Lonnie George Johnson October

6, 1949- present has over 80 patents but you may know him for his creations Nerf 1996 and Super Soakers 1986.

James Edward Maceo West: born Feb., 19, 1931- present he holds over two hundred and fifty U.S. and Foreign patents because of him we can use the camcorders, hearing-aids, baby- monitors, and telephones among other things because of one particular patent for the polymer foil electrets.

Benjamin F. Jackson: patent the gas burner in 1899

James Earl Lewis: antenna feed for coordinating tracking radars

James M. Brooks

Jan Ernst Matzeliger: born September 15, 1852-august 24, 1889) created a shoe making machine that could produce anywhere between 100-700 shoes a hr. in March 1883 calling it the lasting machine.

Andrew Jackson Beard: born 1849-1921) after being emancipated and married he became a farmer and built his first and second invention the plow. Years later he made two improvements patents to the knuckle coupler on trains.

Willis Johnson: patented the egg beater or whisk I like to call it on Feb. 5, 1884

Sarah E. Goode: born Sarah Elisabeth Jacobs 1855- April 8, 1905) Sarah invented the first folding bed. it was actually a folding cabinet bed in July 14. 1885. When folded looked like a desk. She came up with the idea after hearing customers complain about such little space in their homes. Goode was the first African American woman to receive a U.S. patent.

Benjamin Bradley: developed and t an engine large enough to run the first steam powered warship. But because he was a slave he could not get a U.S. patent so he sold his invention kept the money and bought his freedom.

Thomas J. Marshall

Ben Montgomery: born Benjamin Thornton Montgomery 1819-1877 was an inventor who didn't get to patent his creation or improvement creation to boat propellers. Being a slave you were not an U.S. citizen also slave and slave owners could not receive patents on inventions created by slaves. Did you know Montgomery was sold to Joseph Davis the brother of Jefferson Davis the president of the confederate states? It's said that after both of these brothers tried to get patents on Montgomery improvements but failed because they were not the original creators. Jefferson Davis passed the law all slaves could receive U.S. Patents.

In 1857 a slave owner challenged the law saying he reaped the all the fruits of his slaves labor including any inventions. The law changed in 1858 stating slaves were not citizens and could not hold patents. After the civil war the law changed to grant all men not women the rights to patents.

Janet Emerson Bashen: born Feb 12, 1957- present) software program to help with equal employment opportunity investigations.

Anthony "A.L." Lewis

Marjorie Joyner: born Marjorie Stewart Joyner October 24, 1896- December 27, 1994) in 1928 she invented the hot rod rollers or permanent wave. Was one of the first African American woman to receive a U.S. PATENT.

Valerie Thomas Created a 3-D optical illusion device

Robert Roosevelt Brooks

Lloyd Hall: born LLYOD Augustus Hall June 20, 1894- January 2, 1971, in total hall held 59 patents He patents mostly deal with idea of preserving food keeping it from spoiling think of camp packaged foods.

Henry Brown: a safe/locked strongbox on November 2, 1886 it was fire and accident safe with a lock and key an improvement to a previous patent.

Mary Beeatrice Davidson Kenner: born May 17, 1912 the first to patent a sanitary napkin with a belt, toilet paper holder, a shower washer, and a mounted back scrubber.

A slave owner **Stewart** took his slaves patent cotton processing something or other, his name **Ned** is the only thing in reference to him in the patent.

Earl Lucas: twenty four patent improvements to cars and one of the 30 black car designers in the world.

John Parker: born John P. Parker 1827- January 30, 1900) in 1884 patented the tobacco press.

Madeline Turner: the fruit press in April 25, 1916

Emmit McHenry: he is the reason we can surf the net and send out emails. Say hello to the developer Mr. dot com himself.

Gaetano Brooks

Lyda D. Newman on November 15, 1898 her us patent for a bristle hair brush that could be taken apart for efficient cleaning.

Joseph Winters: born Joseph Richard Winters august 29, 1816- November 29, 1916) his first patent was the improvement of a previous wagon-mounted fire escape replacing the wood with metal a couple years later he really upgraded receiving patent for fire escape ladder for buildings.

William Henry Cling: several inventions most related to apparel but my favorite is that for beds that bend upright for people confined to beds for illness.

Annie Malone: born Annie Minerva Turnbo Malone august 9, 1869- May 10, 1957 made hair care products and the developments of mail order process for beauty care products.

Henry Blair: born 1807-1860 October 14, 1834 he patented the seed planter, august 31, 1836 he patented the cotton planter the second African American to receive a patent. He signed his name as X because he was illiterate.

Patricia Bath: born Patricia Era Bath November 4, 1942 owns four patents all catered around helping people with cataracts. She is also the first African American female doctor receiving a patent for medical purpose in 1988.

Anna M. Mangin: pastry fork

Mark Dean: born mark e dean march 2, 1957 co-creator of the IBM computer holding three patents. First African American to become an IBM Fellow, with a co-worker he invented a microcomputer system this invention allows up to use computer plug-ins.

Leonard C. Bailey: Folding bed

Miriam Benjamin: born Mariam Benjamin sept 6, 1861-1947) gong and signal chair on July 17, 1888 think of how you signal for your flight attendant on a plane.

Phil Brooks: disposable syringe

Norbert Rillieux: born March 17, 1806- October 8, 1894) patented a product that pressed sugar out of sugar cane.

Nathaniel Mathis: Barbers Apron

A.W. Martin: the locked door

In 1857 a slave owner challenged the law saying he reaped the all the fruits of his slaves labor including any inventions. The law changed in 1858 stating slaves were not citizens and could not hold patents. After the civil war the law changed to grant all men not women the rights to patents.

Charles S. L. Baker (and possible his brother Peter was involved): Invented the radiator system. Charles also made improvements to the automatic signaling system

Henrietta Bradberry

The concept of a pillow or place to rest head was created in Africa. Seems as if African understood sleep was need to recharge and a way to control the Subconscious mind.

Naturally being human we have our instincts and we all have something that we need or want. When we don't try to pursue to obtain those goals when it is just a thought it will make you become bitter. Because you're holding on to something that was meant to flourish only letting it fester and you begin to feel sorry for yourself. In order to obtain something you have to do something. Look up these patents plus there are many more like DVD's, IPod, remote control, female cycle indicator and predictor,

Netta B.

VCR remote timer, Vchip, photography, cars, guns the list goes on just research.

"The colour of the skin is in no way connected with strength of the mind or intellectual powers."

Benjamin Banneker

MELANIN

Netta B.

NOTES

MELANIN

TRUE OR FALSE

1. Ruby Dee was an Actress, Civil Rights Activist, screenwriter and the well-known for role of Ruth Younger in "Raisin in the Sun"

    TRUE   FALSE

2. Elaine Brown is a Writer, singer, American Prison Activist, former chairwomen for Black Panther Party and supporter of the Green Party.

    TRUE   FALSE

3. Marley Dias created #1000BlackGirlBooks

   TRUE   FALSE

4. Phillis Wheatley first African American woman to publish a book "Poems on Various Subjects, Religious and Moral, from 1773.

   TRUE   FALSE

5. Dr. Yosef Ben Jochannan as a writer and historian unrecognized by mainstream scholars because the authenticity of and in his education.

   TRUE   FALSE

6. Augustus Jackson influenced Ice Cream flavors including the making of it he also served as a Chief in the White House in the 1820s.

   TRUE   FALSE

7. Emmett Chappelle is considered a man of science.

TRUE   FALSE

8. Dr. John Henrik Clarke A pan-Africanist writer and pioneer in the creation of Africana studies.

TRUE   FALSE

9. Robert Henry Lawrence Jr. was the first African American Astronaut also being an Air Force officer.

TRUE   FALSE

10. Amanda Berry Smith was an nationwide renown missionary.

TRUE   FALSE

11. Anala Beevers held a IQ over 145 at the age of

five.

TRUE   FALSE

12. Mrs. F.E.W. Harper refused to give up her seat on a trolley in 1858 Harper was also the first black woman to publish a short story. Harper wrote "Bury Me in a Free Land" and "The Two Offers"

TRUE   FALSE

13. Cicely Tyson has been an actress for almost 70yrs.

TRUE   FALSE

14. Pam Grier could be considered cinemas first female action star.

TRUE   FALSE

15. Tony Hansberry Jr child Jr child prodigy in medicine at age 14 dubbed "The next Charles

Drew"

TRUE   FALSE

16. Oscar Micheaux was an entrepreneur turned film director, independent producer over 40 films, and author.

TRUE   FALSE

17. Nichelle Nichouls played Lieutenant Uhura on "Star Trek" gaining major support and idolism for portraying a colored person as an equal and not a slave.

TRUE   FALSE

18. David Van Valen was accepted to MIT at the age of thirteen.

TRUE   FALSE

19. Sammy Davis Jr is known for hits "I've Gotta Be Me" and "The Candy Man"

TRUE   FALSE

20. Garrett Morgan acting as a "big chief mason" kind of masking his identity to sell his inventions and is also known for using one of his inventions to rescue men out of a tunnel explosion in July 1916.

TRUE   FALSE

21. Wallace D. Fard is the Co-founder of Nation of Islam.

TRUE   FALSE

22. Miles Davis is considered a pioneer of 20th century music.

TRUE   FALSE

23. Ernie Davis was the first African American to win Heisman Trophy in 1961.

TRUE   FALSE

24. Mabou Loiseau is an eight year old genius who knows eight languages and eight instruments.

TRUE   FALSE

25. In Sept 15 1963 four young girls were killed in a church bombing.

TRUE   FALSE

26. In 1957 The little rock nine hand selected group of African Americans teens desegregated Little Rock Central High School.

TRUE   FALSE

27. Fred Hampton was a revolutionary and activist that was killed in his sleep during a home raid.

TRUE   FALSE

28. Kwanzaa is a celebration of cultural heritage and traditional values observed December 26th-January 1st.

TRUE   FALSE

29. Malcom X was killed in front of his children and pregnant wife.

TRUE   FALSE

30. Trevon martin was a seventeen year old fatally shot by a neighborhood watch volunteer whose case caused a nationwide frenzy.

TRUE   FALSE

31. Arthur Ashe was the first African American to win at Wimbledon.

TRUE   FALSE

32. Jeff /Jack Johnson was known as Galveston Giant.

TRUE   FALSE

33. Willie Reed helped bring Emmett Till's death justice by being a key witness.

TRUE   FALSE

34. John Swett Rock is known for coining the term "Black is Beautiful"

TRUE   FALSE

MELANIN

*"I believe people who practice their
beliefs in daily life are activists."*

Jasmine Guy

Netta B.

NOTES

Netta B.

FUN FACTS

At the 1968 Olympics Tommie Smith and John Carlos raised their black gloved fist to the podium while also covering their feet with only black socks representing black poverty in America.

In the 1940's Richard Wright's novel Native Son was the first best-selling African American Novel.

There is a college in Harlem called Malcolm-King College.

Paul Roberson was a singer, athlete, actor, activist, lawyer, author, and scholar your true 20th-century Renaissance man.

Cree Summer Francks is the voice over/voice actress QUEEN.

Nat King Cole first African American to have a variety radio show and host a prime time national syndicate.

Did you know Angela Davis ran for Vice President on the Communist Party twice?

John Morton-Finney practiced law for eighty five years.

Nigeria bobsled team was the first African American team to qualify in the winter Olympics in 2017.

"The Black Cyclone" born Charles W. Follis was the first African American professional football player.

Elmer Simms Campbell first African American nationally published cartoonist.

Mr. T started his neck full of gold chains by working at a bouncer whenever someone lost a chain he would wear it around his neck just in case the person came back looking for it he was a human lost and found.

John Baxter Taylor Jr. was the first African American to

win a Olympic gold medal.

William Wells Brown first African American to publish a novel "Clotel; or, The President's Daughter" in 1853 in 1858 he became the first to publish a play "The Escape; or, A Leap for Freedom"

In 2001 Sheila Johnson was labeled First African American woman billionaire and Robert L Johnson being the first African American man billionaire.

Mansa Masu was an emperor of Mali a West African empire making it the largest and richest in the fourteenth century. Masu was best known for being one of the richest people of all time, and voyage to Mecca in 1324 for prosperity and unity throughout Mali. This made him one of the first African rulers to be known throughout the Middle East and Europe.

Trayvon Martins lawyers wore hoodies in court.

Ceata E. Lash first creator of two patents for the naturalista sista.

Drake donated a recording studio to Strawberry Mansion High School.

The Dahomey Amazons were some of the most feared

women ever.

Frederick Douglas Patterson was America first Black automobile manufactures.

Viola Davis, Lorenz Tate and Kerri Washington are working on their own production companies.

Patricia S. Cowings first woman to be trained as an astronaut.

Colin Kaepernick knelled during the national anthem in 2016 before his NFL football game because he felt there was too much wrong doing toward African Americans and minorities in the States he received a lot of backlash for this not being picked up for a season by any league coining the hashtag "take a knee" only to have later score a book deal and be named GQ Magazine citizen of the year.

George Washington Carver is known for three hundred ways of peanuts but also 75 things for pecans and one hundred eighteen for sweet potatoes.

Emma Frances Grayson Merritt started the first United States Kindergarten for African American students in 1890.

The founders of Spellman College Harriet Giles and Sophia Tucker started with only one hundred dollars.

Bob Marley faced racism and discrimination while growing up due to having a British father.

Jeremiah G. Hamilton was Wall Street's first Black millionaire.

Orrin Cromwell Evans was the first black writer for a mainstream American white newspaper and the very first creator of all black comics he called "The Nergo Comics" in 1947 selling his for fifteen cents instead of ten cents. John Terrell and Evans brother George J Evans Jr. helped with the drawings.

Delores Brown received a dancing scholarship for her ballet at the age of fourteen.

The King and Queen in Coming to America was also the King and Queen voice over actors in the Lion King.

Eartha Pascal Trouillot first Haiti female president and woman lawyer.

Aretha Franklin was the first women to be added to the

Rock and Roll Hall of Fame in 1987.

Gabby Douglas has a doll and it looks just like her.

In 2008 the East African natation Rwanda banned plastic bags virtually making it one of the most liter free countries.

Girl Trip written, produced, directed with an all-star Black cast became the first African American film to surpass one hundred million dollars. As it should the movie was hilarious with an awesome message.

Ramarni Wilfred an 11 yr. old scored higher than Einstein and Bill Gates.

October 6, 1871 Fisk University gospel Jubilee singers started their first national tour to raise money for their school.

Anna Murray-Douglass Frederick Douglass first wife who was born free and a business woman encouraged and helped Douglass obtain his freedom; she also created an Underground Railroad headquarters from her home.

Erin Jackson First Black woman to qualify for the long-track speed skating U.S. Olympic team in 2018.

Daniel Geiter an Ex-felon helped open Higher education for felons to back to school in the south side of Chicago.

"Dr. D." Dorothy Lavinia Brown was the first African American female surgeon.

Wallace "Wally" Amos is not only the creator of Famous Amos Cookies he also is author and TV personality.

Dreadlocks date back far as A.D. 400 when hair naturally matted together and hair instruments were not made yet dreads also represent a symbol and vow not to alter Gods creation in a religious devotion.

Dred Scott born 1799-September 17, 1858 sued for himself and his family and won eventually.

Oscar Micheaux's "Within Our Gates" was the first film produced and directed by an African American.

Trae Tha Truth has a non-profit called Angel by Nature.

Oprah 1993 interview with Michael Jackson is the most watched interview in TV history.

Did you know Prince invited Michael Jordan to work with a company he helped and invested in? That company was Nike.

Chuck Berry the "King of Rock and Roll".

Benjamin F. Ben Hardy was a motorcycle engineer who built the choppers for the movie Easy Rider.

John William Rogan aka Bud was the tallest Black man to date reaching 8'8.

So Soul Food is considered a Native American Cuisine I guess that makes since to me since Indians were Black.

Angelica Jason Sweeting has dolls that are identifiable to Brown skin children called Naturally Perfect Dolls.

Moziah Bridges started a Bow Tie line he founded in 2011 at the age of 9 and now has a contract with the NBA.

African American business woman and teacher Maggie Lena Walker was the first female bank president of any race to charter a bank in the U.S. the St. Luke Penny Savings Bank founded in 1903 now known as the Consolidated Bank and Trust.

Silver Bluff Baptist Church of South Carolina was the first African American church led by David George in 1773.

Bennett College in Greensboro North Carolina is a historically black college for women.

Dido Elizabeth belle a mulatto was said to inspire a number of rulings on slavery from here presence in her uncle's home (fathers side) which was the begging to abolition of slavery in England. The movie "Belle" is loosely based off her story.

Harrison Okene survived in a capsized tugboat for three days by finding an air bubble, he was the sole survivor of 12 people.

Tom Joyner has raised millions of dollars to financially provide for HBCU's, Will and Jada Smith, Denzel Washington, and Blair Underwood are also very big with giving to charities.

Lena Waithe is the first African American woman to win a Emmy for Outstanding Writing for a Comedy Series.

Levi Coffin was the president of the Underground

Railway Tubman was the runner.

Sam Graddy first AA piolet.

Nana Yaa Asantewaa was a Queen, human rights activist, politician, mother and farmer. Asantewaa is known for leading the Ashanti rebellion (Yaa Asantewaa war) against the British to protect the Golden Stool in 1900.
.

Isaac Burns Murphy was a Hall of Fall Jockey and is considered one of the greatest riders in Thoroughbred horse racing history.

Don Hogan Charles was first African American hired by the New York Times acclaimed for iconic shots and being in the middle of the Civil rights movement.

In 1777 Vermont was the first U.S. territory to abolish slavery.

Ernestine Shepherd was known as the oldest competitive female bodybuilder at the age of 73 in 2001.

John Hanson an African American was the very first president of the United States in Congress Assembled under the Articles of Confederation being elected and holding office 1781-1782. He sent silver to George

Washington and troops for shoes. Some research leads to believe Hanson was white. Did you know that black man on the back of the two dollar bill is said to be John Hanson? No wonder those bills are almost extinct. LOL

January 24, 1884 Frederick Douglas married Helen Pitts his second wife which bothered and confused a few people.

Cornealious Michael Anderson III is known as "The Man They Forgot to Lock Up".

Toni Stone one of the first woman to play in the Negro baseball league.

Cheryl Brown won Miss Iowa in 1970 becoming the first Black to compete for Miss America.

Azie Taylor Morton is the first and only African American woman to be Treasurer of the United States holding office Sept. 12, 1977 – Jan. 20, 1981. I have to find one of her bills, just to save. Blanche Kelso Bruce was the first mulatto to have his signature on U.S. Currency in 1881 then again in 1897.

Ed Dwight was the first Black accepted to the Astronaut Program but declined due to discrimination matters.

Alexander Lucius Twilight was born by two mulattos Ichabod and Mary Twilight who were labeled the first African Americans to Corinth Vermont. Alexander was the first African American elected state legislator in 1836 sitting office for 21 yrs. He was also pegged first African American to receive a degree from an American College.

Lovie Yancey was the founder of Fatburger located in South Central L.A. in 1952 separating from her business partners and closing her original hamburger stand Mr. Fatburger.

Charlotte E. Ray first black female lawyer in the U.S. graduated Howard University School of Law in 1872.

Maurice Ashley is an author, puzzle inventor, motivational speaker, commentator, app designer, and chess grandmaster.

Michelle Janine Howard has a lot of first's going on can't name them all lol

A young man by the name of Bobby Hutton was the Treasurer and the very first recruit of the Black Panther Party in 1968.

Michael Jackson drunk his wine from diet coke cans.

Wendell Pierce built homes in the Pontchartrain Park neighborhood of Louisiana after Hurricane Katrina and the mistreatment of the insurance companies including but not limited to his own home, his parents, and their neighbors and plan on building more than just homes in the future maybe after he done with the chain of stores. Bless him.

Velma Scantlebury first African American female transplant surgeon.

Cudjoe Kazoolo Lewis was the last known survivor of the Atlantic slave trade he was taken in 1860 at the age of 19 five years later word got to him and others by union soldiers that they were free.

Jupiter Hammon is the first African American man to be a published author.

Benjamin Banneker Viewed as a genius and the United States first black great inventor. Banneker received a watch as a gift becoming fascinated by it repeatedly took the watch apart then put it back together.

Carolyn Gudger an armed resource officer held a potential gunman at bay until the police arrived to Sullivan Central High School in Tennessee.

Elizabeth Freeman or Mum Bett was the first woman to sue for freedom in 1781 and she won.

1ST Rhode Island Regiment was the first African American U.S. military regiment in 1778.

Sarah Collins now known as Sarah Collins Rudolph is the surviving victim of the Birmingham Church Bombing in 1963 there was five girls in the building.

Flora Stewart hailed one of the oldest to live reaching 118 years of age.

At the age of six Alexis Goggins took six bullets to save her mom and survived.

Did you Know Osborne Perry Anderson was the only African American to survive John Browns raid on Harpers Ferry.

Joseph Jenkins Roberts is said to be the first African American president of any nation. He was elected to be the very first and seventh president of Liberia. Although born in Virginia he migrated to Liberia opening a trading store in Monrovia then later learning or engaging in politics.

Bill "Bojangles" Robinson was one of the highest paid African American entertainers of the first half of the twentieth century and May 25th which is his birthday is National Tap Dance Day.

Prince Whippie and Oliver Cromwell served with and helped George Washington American Revolution crossing the Delaware.

Ida Eisenhower born Ida Stover was a mulatto woman who was the mother of Dwight David Eisenhower the 34th president of the United States. I wonder how many other presidents had African American roots.

Kendra Harrison is the fastest hurdler.

Olaminde Orekunrin is the founder of Flying Doctors Nigeria West Africa's first Air Ambulance Service.

Joseph Hayne Rainey first black to reside over the house of representative.

KRS-One name means Knowledge Reigns Supreme Over Nearly Everyone.

Alexa Irene Canady first African American female

neurosurgeon.

Gracia Ral de Santa Teresa de Mose was the very first "Free" African American community in 1738 which is actually a historic site name Fort Mose in St. Augustine Florida.

Charles Ward Chappelle won a medal for being the only African American to invent and display an airplane at the 1911 First Industrial Airplane Show. He had successfully designed a long distance airplane.

Janet Emerson Bashen is the first African American woman to have a software patent.

Maya Angelou was raped at seven when her rapist was murdered she felt like she caused his death by saying his name. For five years she sat in silence not speaking but while mute she read many books gaining lots of knowledge in how to speak and ways to speak.

Jessie Redmon Fauset was the first black woman accepted to Phi Beta Kappa.

Thomas Mundy Peterson first African American to vote after the 15th Amendment was installed.

The National Council of Negro Women is one of the largest woman organizations.

Ben Carson is the first surgeon to successfully separate craniopagus twins.

Richard Allen first founder of a black denomination in America (AME) he served as a solider in the American Revolution while also thought to be the first man to practice medicine.

Paul Williams learned and mastered the art of drawing upside down so he could sit across white clients that didn't want to sit next to a black person.

Richard Theodore Greener first Black to graduate Harvard and become dean of Howard University.

Jaqueline Kiplimo an elite Kenyan runner slowed down to help a dehydrated Chinese runner who had no hands this slowed her down to win second place instead of the first place and ten thousand dollars cash good people still do exist.

Minnie Joycelyn Elders first African American Surgeon General of the United States.

Interracial marriage was banned in 1664 taking three hundred years to be overturned in 1967 thanks to a famous Supreme Court trial Lovings v. Virginia.

Imhotep was a writer, architect, priest, doctor, and chief official of Pharaoh Djoser whom he created the Step Pyramid of Djoser the first structure created by human hands entirely of stone in 2630-2611 BC in Saqqara Egypt.

Misty Copeland's kids book "The Firebird" is based off of her and Raven Wikinson very own friendship.

Shirley Chisholm's Presidential campaign read "BRING U.S. TOGETHER VOTE CHISHOLM 1972 UNBOUGHT AND UNBOSSED" She was lit loved this when I came across it on the internet.

Louis T. Wright was the first African American on a surgical staff of a non-segregated all white hospital.

Folorunso Alakija one of the most powerful women in Africa was pegged the first Nigerian billionaire being the second richest next to Oprah.

Clark Atlanta University, Spellman College, Howard University, Fisk University, Dillard University, Morehouse College, Tuskegee University, and Hampton

University are considered the Black Ivy League.

Queen Nzinga is known for being one of the strongest and ruthless queens of the seventeenth century. She helped fight against the Portuguese expanding their slave trade in Central Africa. The movie "Njinga, Rainha de Angola" gives you piece of her story.

Magic Johnson owes a cable network Aspire television aimed towards the African American audience.

Garrett Morgan Acted as "big chief mason" to sell his inventions and is also known for using one of his inventions to rescue men out of a tunnel explosion July 1916.

In 1854 the oldest Historically Black University in American Lincoln University was founded, then named Ashmun Institute. Wilberforce University was the first black owned and operated University in 1863.

Eight consecutive years the entire senior class of inner city Chicago all male Urban Prep Academy was admitted into college.

Tennessee was the first state to allow enlistment from all men disregarding color.

David Crosthwait holds eighty international patents and forty United States patents. He wrote an instruction manual and guide for heating and cooling standards and codes that dealt with heating a/c and ventilation.

Will and William West were two inmates with the same name and identical looks they were both being held at the Leavenworth Penitentiary being received in to the system three yrs. apart. These two are said to be the reason behind the fingerprinting system.

Mary Edmonia Lewis first African American Sculptor to receive international fame and recognition.

There is a app called the Black Box and Brown Sugar they are like the "Black" HULU and Netflix.

Pedro Alonso Nino navigated for Christopher Columbus.

Absalom Boston was the first African American to Captain and sail a whaleship with an all-black crew in 1822.

Gabby Douglas first African American to win an individual all-around Olympic gymnastics gold.

George Raveling is known or thought to still have the full original version of "I Have a Dream" Speech in his possession today.

Aaliyah was one of the first R&B singers to secure a modeling contract with a major fashion line which was Tommy Hilfiger.

Carter G Woodson the creator of "Negro Week" now known as Black History Month was the first African American to graduate with a Ph. D from Harvard University.

Earnest Green of the Colorado Nine was the first black person to graduate from Central High School in Little Rock, Arkansas in 1958.

Alabama was the last state to legalize interracial marriage in 2000.

In 1827 John Brown Russwurm and Samuel Cornish started the first Black audience periodical it was called Freedom's Journal.

Victor Blanco was an active Black mayor of San Antonio before slavery was abolished back in 1809.

Queen Amina who was the warrior queen of Zazzau during a thirty four year reign she fought and expanded her kingdom to the greatest in history, boosting it with gold, slaves, and crops. She also introduced her army to armor like iron helmets and chain mail a built protective barriers around her military camps with earthen walls which were later called Amina's walls.

It was said that Mahalia Jackson egged Martin Luther King Jr. on whispering to him "Tell em about the dream!"

James Weldon Johnson wrote "Lift Every Voice and sing" in the 1900's singing it at Abraham Lincoln birthday soon after it became known as the "Negro National Anthem"

Dr. Daniel Hale Williams who received his M.D. in 1883 founded the Provident Hospital in Chicago in 1891 making it the oldest Black owned and ran hospital in the United States.

Brazil was the last country to ban slavery in 1888.

Ida Wells Barnet refused to give up her seat in 1884 and bit a conductor on the hand when tried to pull her off, she was dragged off the trolley were she later sued and won. The win was short lived though.

Bill Cosby was the first African American to star in a television Series "I Spy" in 1965 with his white counterpart.

In 1780 Pennsylvania was the first state to abolish slavery.

Joyce Bryant a 50's era singer sprayed her hair with radiator paint dubbing her "The Bronze Bombshell"

Lincoln University in Pennsylvania was the 1st institution of higher education founded for African Americans (Albert Einstein taught a physics class.)

The reason I believe the reason the Stono Rebellion was such a huge slave revolt is because some of the men were actually soldiers in Africa before they were slaves.

Tice Davids was a runaway slave who swam across the Ohio River to freedom. People thought he died his former owner said "He must of have traveled on an underground railroad" coining the term underground railroad.

Ina Ray Hutton born Odessa Cowan who passed for a white was the leader of Melodears one of the first all-female swinging bands that was filmed and recorded

Quakers were the first recorded to protest slavery in 1688.

Freedoms Journal was the first African American owned and operated newspaper founded in 1827 by Peter Williams and company in New York City.

Col. Guion S. Bluford Jr. first African American in space.

Carl Brashear first African American U.S. Navy Master Diver 1970 while having an amputated leg.

Augustus Jackson Influenced Ice Cream flavors and making of it he also served as a chief in the White House in the 1820s.

Robert Henry Lawrence Jr. was the first African American astronaut, also an Air Force officer.

Calculus, geometry, and trigonometry all trace back to African Scholars. Have you ever heard of Ishango bone? It's just called one of "The Oldest testimonial of numeric calculus is human history."

Haile Selassi's ancestry can be traced back to King Solomon and Queen Sheba some of the most ancient lineage to date.

Jackie Ormes born Zelda Melvin Jackson was the first African American female cartoonist for the newspaper.

Fredi Washington known for her role to play light skinned black women who decides to pass as white, Washington was very active during the Harlem Renaissance.

Kimberly Anyadike is the youngest pilot to single handily fly across the USA.

Eliza Anna Grier first African American woman licensed to practice medicine.

Ruby Bridges was escorted by federal marshals in 1960 into and out of her new elementary school William Frantz Elementary. To this day Rudy still volunteers at her old school were her family have even attends.

Langston Hughes father would only agree to pay for his school if he studied engineering and not becoming a writer.

Netta B.

"We are the ones we've been waiting for."

June Jordan

MELANIN

NOTES

MELANIN

BACK IN THE DAYS

Atlantic slave trade took place from the 15th through 19th century across The Atlantic Ocean where Africans and Israelites where kidnapped and deported to America to work on plantations and mines. Around 7 to 12 million POC where migrated to the Western Hemisphere the voyage from Africa to whatever destination could last anywhere from four to twelve weeks. Men and women were held under in the lower part of the ship packed and separated by sex. Death was high on ships leaving for the ill or deceased to be tossed overboard. Because of the poor environment sickness came easily one of the top illnesses being scurvy. The workout plan was for them to go on top deck and dance. Suicide and revolts were very frequent on these rides.

Interracial marriage also then known as miscegenation was banned in the US in 1616 and was overturned in

1967 Alabama was the last state to legalize interracial marriage in 2000.

The Nation Safe Haven Freedman's Village Va. 1863 the federal government built 50 one and half story houses made for two families each. The government closed down the village in 1900. Now it holds the pentagon, Navy Annex building and some of the Arlington National Cemetery.

Women's suffrage women gained the right to vote nationwide in the 1920's.

Drapetomania was diagnosed by Samuel A. Cartwright as being the urge to flee captivity he said it was an illness to have an irrational desire to be free. This was an illness diagnosed to slaves who just wanted to be free or tried to run away.

Joyland the first amusement park built for African Americans on May 6, 1921 in Fulton county Atlanta Georgia. It is now a small community in southeast Atlanta.

Seneca Village was located between 82nd – 89th street between 7th and 8th avenue in Manhattan New York City made predominant of Black business owners between 1825 -1857. The area was destroyed leaving an estimate of 300 people homeless it is now known as central park.

Black Wallstreet Greenwood, Oklahoma or Tulsa race riot On June 1, 1921 in Greenwood, Oklahoma the first ever bombing on America soil took place. On May 31 1912 word got out that a black man was accused of raping a white female elevator operator during a Memorial Day weekend. Rumors spread throughout the community that he was going to be lynched a group of armed black men went to protest and help prevent a lynching outside the police station the young men was held. A confrontation between blacks and white ensued shots were fired and both blacks and whites were killed. The news of what happened spread and that night and next day a mob tore through the Greenwood community killing men and women, burning and looting homes and businesses. Black Wall Street was attacked from the air on June 1, 1921 by falling sticks of dynamite and burning balls of turpentine, Destroying over 600 black owed businesses and homes that included schools hospitals church's grocery stores banks etc. literally their life.

Children's Crusade in Birmingham thousands of teens and young people got together to participate in a non-violent demonstrations in May of 1963.

Ethnological expositions also known as human zoo or Negro villages took place in the 19th and 20th century where there were public exhibitions of people of the African Asian and indigenous people decent where it appeared they were in their natural state of surroundings. The last know exhibit was in Belgium circa 1958. Some names that may pop into mind when you read the description are The Muse Brothers, Saartjie Sarah Baartman, Ota Benga and the McCoy twins to name a few.

Weeksville now known as Bedford-Stuyvesant, Brooklyn New York was land that a freedmen James weeks bought from another freedmen named Henry C. Thompson.

Weeks sold some property to other free blacks it became the home to southern black escaping slavery and northerners escaping racial violence or prejudice. The community soon named after Weeks. It thrived for years.

Jim Crow or Jim Crow Laws was a racial cast system that ran from 1877 through 1965 it was to keep the POC a second class citizen with anti-black laws. The belief was all whites were superior to blacks in all ways including intelligence, civility, and morality it was a goal to keep POC at the bottom of racial hierarchy. Jim Crow gave states a legal way to ignore constitutional obligations to black citizens. Treating blacks as equals would encourage interracial unions and relations and that was thought to destroy America. Violence was instrumental for Jim Crow the justice system was all white and violation of the rules and regulation could end in loss of homes, jobs, and life.

Etiquette

1. White drivers had the right-of-way at all intersections.
2. Blacks were introduced to whites not whites to blacks.
3. Blacks were not allowed to show public affection towards each other in public, because it offended whites.
4. Black males could not offer to light the cigarette of a white woman, it implied intimacy.

5. Blacks had to use courtesy titles of respect when referring to whites (Miss, Ma'am, Mr., Sir) they were not allowed to call them by their first name.
6. If riding with a white person blacks sat in the back.
7. Blacks and whites could not eat together and whites were served first.
8. A black man could not offer to shake hands with a white man because it implied being socially equal.

Laws (I'll do one law example for a couple of states. The reason I'm only doing a few is because throughout the states the main concern was separation and not mixing races, which was the just of the Jim Crow era)

1. Georgia: All persons licensed to conduct the business of selling beer or wine shall serve either white people exclusively or colored people exclusively and shall not sell to the two races within

the same room at any time.
2. California: {Statute} Education African and Indian children must attend separate schools. A separate school would be established upon the written request of parents of ten such children. "A less number may be provided for in separate schools in any other manner."
3. Florida: "Any black man and white man, or any white man and/or Negro woman, who are not married to each other, who shall habitually live in and occupy in the nighttime the same room shall each be punished by imprisonment not exceeding twelve months, or by fine not

exceeding five hundred dollars.
4. Kentucky: (This state had maybe one of the longest list of rules as far as my search went.) Recreation 1956: All business were prohibited from permitting any dancing, social functions, entertainments, athletic training, games, sports or contest on their premises in which the participants are members of the White and African American race.
5. Oklahoma: Funerals {Statute} Blacks were not allowed to use the same hearse as whites.
6. Tennessee: Race classification 1932 {State Code} Classified "Negro" as any person with any African blood.

Lynching or lynch law a method of social control they were public murders carried out by mobs, one of the most extreme forms of Jim Crow methods of violence directed towards black people. It was a way to keep freed people in their place there are about 5,000 known cases of lynching between the late 1800's to mid-1900's most cases were because a black man was accused of rape of a white woman and they had to keep the white woman away from black rapist and the many violent crimes white people said blacks were prone of doing. Most lynchers did not get arrested or convicted of a crime.

Separate but equal happened after the end of the reconstruction era where the federal government made a general policy to let individual states decide its own racial segregation. As long as the facilities provided to each were equal everything could still be segregated by race.

Black Codes laws passed by Southern states in 1865-1866 were actually revisions of slave codes designed to regulate the lives of former slaves. Black codes allowed certain rights like, property ownership (limited), make contracts, legalized marriage, and testify in court. They also denied rights to testify against whites, votes, serve on juries or start jobs without the employer approval. Some state required you sign a year-long labor contract or take the change of vagrancy, forced labor, or arrest.
- A. Employment was required of all freedmen
- B. Freedmen were not to be taught to read or write
- C. Public facilities were segregated
- D. Freedmen could not assemble without the presence of a white person
- E. Freedmen were assumed to be agricultural workers and their duties and hours were regulated

 F. Violators could be whipped or branded

This was the basis of Black Codes even though Southern states carried their own due justice on their states Freedmen. It was rough.

Slave Codes were made so slave owners could control and retrieve their slaves from free states different states had state laws that included the definition of a slave, slaves reading, when death and whippings or okay, rules on freeing slave. Just rules, rules, and rules, and you thought the Jim Crow and Black codes were strict.

Confederate states: states that unrecognized breakaway whose regional economy was dependent on slaves for their agricultural labor in cotton picking and whatever plantation work. 1861-1865 the original seven South Carolina, Mississippi, Florida, Georgia, Louisiana, and Texas later Tennessee, Virginia, North Carolina, and Arkansas were added.

Barrel of laughs: back in the days slave owners found it disrespectful for slaves to laugh in their presence so some slave owners had barrels set up for the purpose of a slave finding something funny they could go to the barrel as if getting something coming back up with a straight face. This is beyond ridiculous to me.

MOVE was a black liberation group founded by John Africa in 1972. Its sole purpose was to engage in public demonstrations against police brutality and racism. The group lived communally in a row house In Philadelphia. After a standoff with the police in 1985 the Philadelphia Police Department flew a helicopter dropping two bombs onto their compound causing a fire that burst out of control taking 65 homes under the order of let the fire burn. People ran out of burning houses were shot dead or shot at leaving them to return back into burning house. John Africa and ten others five adult five children died as a result of that fire and over 200 were left homeless. Go check out the documentary Let the Fire Burn.

Race Riots They usually carry the some of the same traits of starting in the black community a white person is initiating a confrontation, police can sometimes agitate or side with the attacker, rumors or hear say play a big role. Examples below

        New York Race Riot 1863
        Red Summer 1919
        Toledo Riot 2005
        Overtown Riot 1989
        Rosewood Massacre 1923
        Tulsa OK Massacre 1912
        Orangeburg Massacre 1968
        Washington DC Race Riots 1919
        Los Angeles Riots 1992
        East St Louis Massacre 1917
        Opelousas Massacre 1868
        Atlanta race Riot 1906
        Camden Riot 1971
        Knoxville TN Race Riot 1919
        Ferguson Unrest 2014/2015

Million Man March took place on October 16, 1995 in Washington D.C. It was a gathering of African American men called to happen by Louis Farrakhan. The group of people from the likes of Nation of Islam, NAACP, and other civil rights organizations. Its purpose was to unite in self-help and self-defense against economic and social ills harboring the African American community.

Browder v. Gayle a trial that blossomed during the Montgomery Bus Boycott in December 1955. It's amazing that a child started it all because she believed in right and wrong. Research and find out how this case ended segregation on busses in Montgomery only in a year time. But why do we still run to the back of the bus?

"Day of Absence" which was to coincide with the Million Man March for those who could not attend the march. On this specific day all African Americans were encouraged to stay home away from their regular day work, school, hobbies, and social events and instead attend worship services and teach-ins focusing on building a healthy and self-sufficient community.

Tuskegee Airmen Experiment Tuskegee Airmen or red tails/red tails angels were the first African American aviators. From 1932 to 1972 the U.S health service conducted an experiment on mainly sharecroppers of Alabama 399 infected men of syphilis and 201 who did not have the disease. Ultimately these men believed they were being treated for bad blood and would receive cure or treatment for any ailments found in the body, free health care, burial insurance, and meals. The study was nothing more but to see how long you would live and if there were different effects in a black and white person. Penicillin became a known cure and still they fail to treat the patients. This experiment concluded with man men how passed, 40 wives who gained the disease, and nineteen kids born with congenital syphilis. Someone who told of the illegal treatment of the study in 1972 help led to changes in U.S. regulations and law studies now require informed consent, reporting of test results and communication of diagnosis.

Slave Rebellion I would say there has to be about a hundred slave rebellions give or take I really don't know. Basically what happened is just a handful of slaves or so gets to together and rebel using force, power in numbers, and determination to turn their current situation better. Some of you may know Nat Turners story, The Haitian Revolution, or Stono Rebellion just to name a few.

Pan-Africanism Movement encourages people to strengthen the bond between people of African descent to know and learn your roots.

Freedom Summer (Mississippi Summer Project) in June 1964 a campaign was held to attempt to register as many African American voters as possible in the state of Mississippi only 5.3 percent of African American were registered.

Harlem Renaissance from the 1920-1930 was an artistic, intellectual, cultural, and social explosion that took place in Harlem New York drawing all creative minds together known then as the "New Negro Movement" filled with music, artist, writers, performers anyone with a vision to progress and the will to not be beat or silent.

Million Woman March took place on October 25, 1997 IN Philadelphia, Pennsylvania. It was underground organized by Phile Chionesu also known as Dr. Phile'. She had an all-star cast of speakers at her event and the day was filled with scheduled hours of prayer speeches and music. The actual attendance is still at question but reports have been made to 300,000 – one million. The women of the march called for three things A. repentance for the pain of black woman caused by one another B. resurrection of African American families and community bonds C. restoration but the ultimate mission was for African American Women to be self-determined.

Freedmen's Bureau was created to assist freedmen after the Civil War it was established March 3, 1865 by Abraham Lincoln. Its purpose was to bring back separated freedmen during and before the war. It extended out teaching freedmen to write read and to work on plantations as employees under contract verses slaves. After Lincoln's assassination the bureau effectiveness and purpose faded a few years later.

Slavery: 1. A condition compared to that of a slave in respect of exhausting labor or restricted freedom. 2. A person who is the legal property of another and forced to obey them.
Gay white men bought male slaves to force homosexual sex. Sodomizing grown men in front of their wife kids family and friends. Homosexuality came from Europeans not Africans Moors taught Europeans how to bathe and practice self-hygiene

Reparations for Slavery well did you know in 1865 General William Tecumseh Sherman ordered 400,000 acres of land to be confiscated along Florida, Georgia, and South Carolinas Atlantic Coast under the Special

Field Orders No. 15. The land was intended to settle 18,000 freed slaves, and freedmen families. Shortly after the then President Lincoln was assassinated his succor Andrew Johnson reversed the order and returned the land to its previous owners. In 1867 Thaddeus Stevens sponsored a bill for the redistribution of land to African Americans, it still has not passed. Read up on Thaddeus Stevens he was a cool little dude.
Why do I believe reparations is due because no one has a bill of sale for any of the people they "owned" so somebody was stealing and kidnapping and owe someone.

Fugitive Slave Act a law requiring all escaped slaves are to be returned home to their original owner. No one could harbor hide a slave without punishment.

The Devils Punchbowl in Natchez Mississippi

King assassination riots also known as **the Holy Week Uprising** riots took place in over one hundred cities all across the United States soon after the assassination of Dr. Martin Luther King Jr. on April 4, 1968 riots lasting a day others lasting multiple days. Dozens died thousands injured and arrested. In the end I believe it was a turning point. A week after king's death the Fair Housing Act was signed and passed.
On August 28, 1963 Martin Luther king gave his I have a dream speech during his march on Washington for jobs and freedom. **200,000 PEOPLE OF ALL RACES AGE AND NATIONALITIES WERE PRESENT**

Willie Lynch Letter a speech William Lynch delivered to an audience on the river bank of the James River in Virginia on 1712. It is said to be the secret to controlling black slaves by placing them against one another. The documents has said to be in print since 1970 but gained widespread notice when it appeared on the internet in 1990's

Willie Lynch Letter secret to controlling back slaves by setting them against each other

Light skinned against dark woman against men they disliked us so much they craved for our separation so we could break each other down which kind of dismantles ourselves within taking inspiration and hope and drain it from us. They know how powerful, athletic, high stamina and strong minded we are. Who better to end someone better than themselves, because if they tried to they would lose, It's called sabotage. When you want to be sneaky hurt someone without them or anyone else knowing it what do you do set traps to make or entice others to do your dirty work so you can sit back and watch.

The black women have attitudes theory. Women are targeted also just not in a violent or direct way. We are targeted through our men that may make us feel small, un-pretty, or just foolish. We crave love and appreciation and when we don't get it we act up or seek it through someone or thing else. Everyone knowns a Black King and Queen together is very powerful and uplifting. Separated we're just confused lost bitter and hateful. I sure you get my drift yes I believe all our self-hate it all comes from the Willie Lynce letter. So with that being said, something that really makes me mad is when a black man or woman dates outside their race for the simple fact they believe their not as attractive because of the dark skin tone or because the stereotype blacks are crazy and or deep rooted issues/attitudes, that's pretty much everyone on the planet nobody is perfect and everyone has something crazy or different going on about them.

I know a lot of you can look at what I write and think what are you talking about we not in that era this is a new era new ways new, new, new. But look around that's a lie the only thing that has changed is technology, fashion, and foods lol. You got to remember there are still a lot of older people 60 and up maybe 50s that seen that hate between the races that experienced it firsthand. People who were taught by parents and grands freed slaves with mentality that was taught on the plantation or act of disrespect that shown in front of them or their family. If they still harbor that and wear it on their sleeve how can racism be gone because that time of protest separate but equal was not very long ago. Forty five to fifty years ago most whites didn't want to integrate most of those people are still alive today people say that was so long ago yes it was a long time ago but it can't die when people that support that thinking and believe in it may still teaching or showing it to today's youth.

Let's Make a Slave or the making of a slave The Willie Lynch Letter is just what Frederick Douglas called it out to be years ago a scientific process of man and spirit breaking it's a process that leaves one lost uncertain and angry.

The Little Rock Nine 1957 was a group of nine African American students enrolled in Little Rock Central High School a previously all white school the NAACP registered nine students in the school based off of excellent grade and attendance. The nine students were Ernest Green, Elizabeth Eckford, Jefferson Thomas, Terrence Roberts, Carlotta Walls Lier, Minnijean Brown, Melba Pattillo Beals. Ernest was the first African American to graduate from Central High School. All the nine took their own challenge look them up and see find, you may even find a movie too.

Memorial Day was founded by former slaves on May 1st 1865 in Charleston SC to honor 257 dead union soldiers who had been buried in mass grave in a confederate prison camp. It took two weeks to dig up the bodies and give them a proper burial.

Juneteenth is what some black folks may consider their independence day. June 19th 1865 when it was announced by Major General Gordon Granger and his troops in Galveston Texas, that all enslaved persons were now free, this took place two and a half years after the Emancipation Proclamation. It's not a federal Holiday Some of the biggest Juneteenth celebrations are held in Milwaukee and Minneapolis.

In **1841 the ship Creole** which soon became known as the Creole case was the result of a successful slave revolt. Rebels who had been taken against their will fought back taking over their ship and directing it to Nassau. Two people died during this revolt one slave and one slave trader. It was considered the most successful revolt in US History with La Amistad being the next successful revolt even though it happened a year earlier in 1839 there was more bloodshed and the surviving crew tricked the slaves at night by traveling in a different direction. The one thing these two cases had in common was the accused had a fair trial and in both favors the court ruled the Africans were entitled to take whatever measure necessary to secure their freedom including force.

NAACP National Association for the Advancement of Colored People: is to ensure the political, educational, social, and economic equality of the rights of all persons and to eliminate race-based discrimination. Founded in Feb 12, 1909 by Mary White Ovington, Moorfield Storey, and W.E.B. Du Bois, it's known to be one of the largest Organizations to date.

Black History Month was founded by Carter G Woodson beginning as just "negro History Week" but in 1976 it became a month long celebration. February was chosen with Frederick Douglas and Abraham Lincoln birthdays in mind.

Nation of Islam (NOI) is a political and religious movement found by Wallace D. Fard Muhammad in Detroit, Mich. On July 4, 1930. It's often call an anti-Semitic or black supremacist group yet their ultimate goal is to improve the spiritual, social, mental, and economic condition of African Americans in the United States and Everywhere else. **Motto:** "Justice or Else!"

Prince Hall was founder of **Prince Hall Freemasonry** in 1775 (PHA) is the first historically Black Fraternal Organization for and composed predominantly of African Americans that were denied the membership of Freemason. It is known as a CHI Rho Fraternity Inc. The original Black Skulls and Cross Bones Fraternity. This is an exclusive invitation only organization. Sister organization **Eastern Stars**

Improved Benevolent Protective Order of Elks of the World (IBPOEW) founded 1897

Historically black colleges and universities (HBCU) were created after the civil war with the intent to serve African American community but has always accepted all races. Lincoln University 1854 and Cheyney University of Pennsylvania 1837 were established before-hand as early as 1837. There are 107 HBCU in the U.S.

Sigma Pi Phi is the first oldest and successful African American incorporated Greek letter organization founded in Philadelphia Pennsylvania May 15, 1904 by four black professionals two doctors, physician and a dentist. It's highly exclusive and known as "the Boule'." Meaning "a council of noblemen" it has a membership of about 5,000.

Social Fellowships **Groove Phi Groove** founded in October 12, 1962 by a group of black men with the purpose of promoting academic awareness, alleviating economic and social disadvantages in the community and teaching traditions incorporating afro centric perspective. **Motto:** "Through loyalty and integrity, we shall achieve greatness." **Swing Phi Swing** non-profit social fellowship founded on April 4, 1969 a fellowship of women committed to community service, achieving and promoting academic excellence, and strengthen community involvement and engagement through culturally conscious activities and events. **Motto:** "Perseverance and Virtue"

The National Pan-Hellenic Council (NPHC) also

called the "Divine Nine" is nine historically African American Organizations working together that was formed as a permanent organization May, 10, 1930 a time when racial segregation ruled and these member decided to stand up against hardships and not accept a state of inferiority. The founding members where Kappa Alpha Psi, Zeta Phi Beta, Omega Psi Phi, Alpha Kappa Alpha, and Delta Sigma Theta a year later Alpha Phi Alpha and Phi Beta Sigma joined, seven years later Sigma Gamma Rho joined and in 1997 Lota Phi Theta joined. **The organizations purpose and mission** "Unanimity of thought and action as far as possible in the conduct of Greek letter collegiate fraternities and sororities, and to consider problems of mutual interest to its member organizations."

Alpha Phi Alpha: Garrett Morgan

Zeta Phi Beta: Annie Turnbo Malone

Sigma Gamma Rho: Kelly Price, Hatti McDaniel

Delta Sigma Theta 1913: Angela Bassett honorary member, Ruby dee, Cicely Tyson

Phi Beta Kappa: Alain Leroy Locke

Alpha Kappa Alpha: Alice coachman honorary member
Kappa Alpha Psi: Marvin Sapp, Horace Mann Bond

Omega Psi Phi: Charles R Drew, Langston Hughes, Bill Crosby, Henry T Sampson

Gamma Phi (march 1, 1905)

Sigma Pi Phi: first and oldest Black Greek Organization (May 15, 1904) W.E.B. Du Bois, Andrew young, John Baxter Taylor Jr, Eric Holder, Ralph Bunche, Ron Brown

Price Hall: garret Morgan

Black Student Union: BSU created in the late 1960s

Black Student Movement: Created November 1967 after disengaging with the NAACP Chapter at the University of North Carolina. **Mission:** We, the members of the Black Student Movement, embrace a culture distinct from the dominant culture found at the University of North Carolina at Chapil Hill. In view of this fact, it is the goal of this organization to strive for the continued existence of the unity among all its members, to voice the concerns and grievances of its members to the University, to offer outlets for expressing Black ideals and culture, and finally, to insure that the Black Student Movement members never lose contact with the Black community."

The Student Nonviolent Coordinating Committee (SNCC) 1960-1976. This group was inspired by Nashville sit-ins. So this group main focus were non-violent organized sit-ins specifically white only lunch counters, which turned to organized protest at segregated public places.

The five-Percent Nation (NGE, NOGE, The Nation of Gods and Earths) founded in 1964 in Harlem New York City by Clarence 13X. his group doesn't consider themselves activist or religion just a lifestyle Supreme

Mathematics, Supreme Alphabets, and One Hundred and Twenty Degrees lesson.

Tenets;

1. That Black people are the original people of planet earth
2. That Black people are the fathers and mothers of civilization
3. That the science of Supreme Mathematics is the key to understanding man's relationship to the universe
4. Islam is a natural way of life not a religion
5. That education should be fashioned to enable us to be self-sufficient as a people
6. That each one should teach one according to their knowledge
7. That the black man is God and his proper name is ALLAH arm, leg, leg, arm, head
8. That our children are our link to the future and they must be nurtured, respected, loved, protected, and educated.
9. That the unified black family is the vital building block of the nation.

Congress of Racial Equality (CORE) Founded in 1942. Some may know the term freedom rides a little better. CORE had a major event May 1961 in the 1960 segregation was ruled to be banned so in May 1961 seven black teens along with seven white teens took a freedom ride on two buses to New Orleans from Washington D.C. In Alabama the kids were attacked and one bus even firebombed. They still continued via an escort. In September the same yr. Interstate commerce commission ruled all passengers should be seated disregard race.

African-American cotillions/debutante balls began in the eighteenth century by French royalty and found its way to the states in the 20th century adopted by wealthy southern whites and some affluent black families. In the 1940s black sororities, frats and social organizations grabbed on to the practice The goal was to introduce young girls to society as well as family business hoping her husband may find her while the young men were seen as being the next top leaders or business men in the community weeks of preparation for these young adults be presented to your community or society learning etiquette, how to dress, dance routines, and manners. There may still be things like this available to our your search key words like debutantes, beautillion, men of tomorrow.

Black Panthers Party also called the BBP originally called the Black Panther Party for Self-Defense. BBP was founded by Huey P. Newton in 1966. Its members started and grew tremendously in California spreading across the states and over the water to the United Kingdom and Algeria. BPP main focus was to challenge and monitor police brutality and behavior to its citizens. BPP was very active in its community mainly providing food for low income children and community health care clinics. Some saw them as a threat some seen them as protection. Dental care, breakfast for low income children, free shoe program, drama classes, and martial arts, at least fifty plus different programs for the community. Each member had twenty six rules which the Black Panther Party followed.

10 Point Program (By Huey P Newton and Bobby Seale

Black Panther Party Self Defense Oct 15, 1966)

What We Want; What We Believe

1. WE WANT FREEDOM. WE WANT POWER TO DETERMINE THE DESTINY OF OUR BLACK COMMUNITY; We believe Black people will not be free until we are able to determine our own destiny
2. WE WANT FULL EMPLOYMENT FOR OUR PEOPLE; We believe that the federal government is responsible and obligated to give every man employment or a guaranteed income. We believe if the white men will not give employment, the means of production should be taken from the businessmen and placed in the community so that the community can organize and employ all of its people and give a high standard of living.
3. WE WANT AN END TO THE ROBBERY BY THE CAPITALIST OF OUR BLACK AND OPPRESSED COMMMUNITIES; We believe that this racist government has robbed us and now we are demanding the overdue debt of forty acres and two mules. Forty acres and two mules were promised 100 years ago as restitution for slave labor and mass murder of Black people. We will accept the payment in currency which will be distributed to our many communities. The American racist has taken part in the slaughter of our fifty million Black people. Therefore, we feel this is a modest demand we make.
4. WE WANT DECENT HOUSING, FIT FOR THE SHELTER OF HUMAN BEINGS; We

believe that if the landlords will not give decent housing to our Black communities, then housing and the land should be made into cooperative so that the people in our communities with government aid can build and make decent housing for the people.

5. WE WANT DECENT EDUCATION FOR OURBPEOPLE THAT EXPOSES THE TRUE NATURE OF THIS DECADENT AMERICAN SOCIETY. WE WANT EDUCATION THAT TEACHES US OUR TRUE HISTORY AND OUR ROLE IN THE PRESENT DAY SOCIETY; We believe in an educational system that will give to our people knowledge of the self. If he/she do not have knowledge of self and your position in the society and in the world then they will have little chance to knowing anything else.

6. WE WANT ALL BLACK MEN TO BE EXEMPT FROM MILITARY SERVICES; We believe Black people should not be forced to fight in the military service to defend the racist government that does not protect us. We will not fight nor kill other people of color in a world who like Black people are being victimized by the white racist government of America. We will protect ourselves from the force and violence of the racist police and the racist military, by whatever means necessary.

7. WE WANT AN IMMEDIATE END TO POLICE BRUTALITY AND MURDER OF BLACK PEOPLE; We believe we can end police brutality in our black community by organizing Black self-defense groups that are dedicated to defending our Black community from racist

police oppression and brutality. The second Amendment of the Constitution of the United States allows us the right to bear arms. Therefor we believe all Black People should arm themselves for self-defense.
8. WE WANT FREEDOM FOR ALL BLACK MEN HELD IN FEDERAL, STATE, COUNTRY AND CITY PRISONS AND JAILS; We believe all Black people should be released from the many jails and prisons because they haven't received an impartial and fair trial.
9. WE WANT ALL BALCK PEOPLE WHEN BROUGHT TO TRAIL TO BE TRIED IN COURT BY A JURY OF THEIR PEER GROUP OF PEOPLE FROM THEIR BLACK COMMUNITIES, AS DEFINED BY THE CONSTITUTION OF THE UNITED STATES; We believe the courts should follow the United States Constitution so that Black people will receive a fair trial.
10. WE WANT LAND, BREAD, HOUSING, EDUCATION, CLOTHING, JUSTICE, AND PEACE

Blaxploitation/blacksploitation films that grew in the 1970s set in poor urban neighborhoods a lot of racial undertones and slurs and often dealt with slavery and miscegenation. Mainly all black cast and where the first to feature a soundtrack filled with soul and funk music.

African Blood Brotherhood to serve as a self-defense organization for blacks threatened by race riots and lynching.

National Negro Business League now called the **National Business League** founded by Booker T. Washington was to promote financial and commercial development of African American Business. Composed and recognized of Black business men and women who were successful business workers. Founded in 1900 gaining more than 600 chapters by 1915.

Brown vs Board of Education is a case that segregation in public schools was unconstitutional since all schools were supported by taxpayers. Linda Brown of Topeka KS Felt she shouldn't have to walk over dangerous route to her all black school when another school even though all white was right in her neighborhood.

Black Liberation Army was an underground organization that ran from 1970-1982. Led by Assata Shakur and Eldridge Cleaver. It got big when the BPP movement died down. Their purpose was to take up arms for the liberation and self-determination of black people in the United States. They were heavily armed and very dangerous. It was said they committed robberies, murders, prison breaks and bombings. Sometimes I think the old movie Dead Presidents has something to do with this group. Just a thought.

Slavery any term, any system in which principle of property law are applied to people.

Mulatto a person of mixed white and black ancestry

Abolitionist advocate/supporter to end slavery or any practice harmful to society.

Statesman a senior politician A notable person who had a long and respected career at a national or international level.

Abolitionism was the movement before and during the American Civil War to end slavery in the United States. It was set to end the Atlantic Slave trade and set slaves free.

Indentured slave a person under contract to work a set amount of time for exchange of something.

Rastafari A African based religion that developed in Jamaica in 1930s after the coronation of Haile Selassie the Emperor of Ethiopia. It became popular in 1970s with Bob Marley making the practice known.

Miscegenation is interbreeding, mixing of different racial groups

Term **Uncle Tom** often used towards a black man considered to be excessively obedient or servile

Underground Railroad secret routes and safe houses used by slaves to escape to free states or Canada

Freedmen an emancipated slave

Civil rights Activist leader of political movement dedicated to securing equal opportunity for members of minority groups Civil rights activist someone working for or against social injustice.

The National Council of Negro Women (NCNW) founded in 1935 by Mary McLeod Bethune. NCNW is a non-profit organization geared towards advancement in opportunities and the quality of life for African-American women, families, and communities.

Inkwell southern California 1905-1965 was the beach for black folks back in the day. In 2008 City of Santa Monica officially recognized "inkwell" and Nick Gabaldon the first African/Mexican decent with a monument and historic landmark at Oceanfront walk and Bay Street.

Black Power is a political name and slogan it's aimed at achieving self-determination for people of African descent. It was first used as such by The then Stokely Carmichael later to be known as Kwame Ture when he stated, "This is the twenty-seventh time I have been arrested and I aint goin to jail no more! The only way we gonna stop them white men from whuppin us is to take over. What we gonna start sayin now is Black Power."

Well known thriving black business districts (founded)

- Black Bottom/Paradise Valley- Detroit Michigan (1960's)
- Harlem (HARLEM RENAISSANCE)- New York (1920's)
- The Ville- St. Louis, Missouri (1860's))
- Historic Central Avenue- Los Angeles (1915)
- Scratch Ankle- Birmingham, Alabama (1972)
- India Avenue- Indianapolis, Indiana (1820's)
- Bronzeville District- South side of Chicago, Illinois (1980's)
- Jackson Ward (The Deuce)- Richmond, Virginia

(1940's)
- 18th and Vine District- Kansas City (1920's)
- Greenwood (Black Wall Street)- Tulsa Oklahoma (1900's)
- Hayti District, Parish Street Black Wall Street- Durham, North Carolina (late 1800's)
- Auburn Ave-Atlanta Ga. (1865)
- U Street- Washington D.C. (1920's)
- Walnut Street Historic District- Louisville Kentucky (1900's)

POC people of color, persons of color: a term to that encompasses all non-white people. People of color made wide circulation in 1970's in the states taking over condescension filled terms non-white and minority.

"Quietly endure, silently suffer and patiently wait."

Martin Luther King Jr.

MELANIN

NOTES

Netta B.

STUMBLED ON THE INTERNET

Huey Freeman a character off of the Boondocks is named after Huey P Newton one of the co-founders of Black Panther Movement. Huey's voice and Riley voice is played by Regina King.

Many have said Avatar is based off the European invasion of Africa how they pushed out of their homeland for mining and studying its past, symbols and traditions but not sharing it with us.

I don't know the truth to this but it's out there that Mozart was a moor. I can't find anything that really makes me believe this but maybe you can.

Martin Luther King Jr. family filed a wrongful death lawsuit in 1999 and won

August 28 2017 the story of an 8 year young Biracial boy

Netta B.

in New Hampshire

According to the 1958 Journal of Social Psychology Black infants develop sooner than other infants

2017 a video surface where a Black man was being sold for four hundred dollars by smugglers auction in Libya this story received very little press.

Do you know what Fluoride does to the mind and body? It is in our water and toothpaste.

Were the first republicans black? Yes. The first blacks in Congress were all Republicans there were no black Democrats till 1935 when Authur Wergs Mitchell an Illinois Democrat rep. Democrats voted against the Civil Rights Act, passed Jim Crow Laws, opposed 13 and 15 amendments, and did you know Democrat John F Kennedy wiretapped Republican Martin Luther King Jr phone. The Republican party founded in 1850's formed primarily of northern white protestants, professionals, businessmen, small- business owners, factory workers, blacks, and farmers it was built with abolishing slavery in mind and expansion on foreign policy. During the Great Depression many voters switched allies between the two parties.

"Django" is based off a real life cowboy Dangerfield Newby. Newby was a freedman who had been free by his white father. After being free he joined John Browns raiders to collect money to buy his wife and children freedom. After collecting the money agreed upon his wife's master took the price higher up. October 17 1859 Newby was killed at Harpers Ferry on his dead body a

letter was found from his wife.
Brentville, August 16, 1859.

Dear Husband.
I want to tell you to buy me as soon as possible for if you do not get me somebody else will. The servants are very disagreeable. They do all that they can to set my mistress against me. Dear Husband you are not the trouble I see these last two years. It has been like a trouble dream to me. It is said that the Master is in want of money. If so I know not what time he may sell me. Then all my bright hopes of the future are blasted. For there has been one bright hope to cheer me in all of my troubles, that is to be with you. For if I thought I should never see you on this earth, life would have no charm for me. Do all you can for me which I have no doubt you will. I want to see you so much. The children are all well. The baby cannot walk yet. The baby can step around anything by holding on to it, very much

Like Agnes. I must bring my letter to a close as I have no news to write. You must write soon and say when you think you can come.

Your' affectionate Wife
HARRIET NEWBY

Ever heard of Isom Dart or better known as the Ned Huddleston story

Have you ever heard of HAARP

Ghetto: (Beginning/ formerly, in most European countries) a section of a city in which all Jews were required to live. Definition: a section of a city, especially a thick populated slum area, inhabited predominantly by members of an ethnic or other minority group, often as a result of social or economic restrictions, pressures, or hardships. So I'm guessing we calling people broke when we use the term ghetto.

Xena the Warrior Princess (television series) was based off of Amina the Warrior Queen of Zazzau, what's now known as Zaria. (SN I used to love Xena she was a real bad ass I could watch episode after episode over and over)

Kheris is a ten year old who started her own tee-shirt line "Flexin In My Complexion"

Curtis Carroll taught himself to read and finance later mastering the stock all while in market while in prison.

Lil Jon teamed up with Pencils of Promise a non-profit and is working on opening a second primary school in Ghana

Do you know what cultural appropriation is?

Stephanie Lampkin founded Blendor a job app that hides race, gender, name and identity only reveling their very relevant matching professional and educational job credentials.

Mumia Abu-Jamal still in jail and still writing books and changing lives. #FreePrince

Three the Hard Way was a 1974 Blaxploitation film about a white supremist tainting part of the city water supply to be lethal to blacks but harmless to white folks. *Sound familiar things that make you go hmm lol*

George Jackson founded The Black Guerilla Family (BGF) in 1966

Be a social advocate for social injustice.

Cathay Williams is the first African American female to enlist and serve in the U.S. Army, only female buffalo solider. She presented herself as a man named William Cathay on Nov 15, 1866 not wanting to stick around during the great depression or depend on others. Only her cousin and one other friend in her same regiment knew of her identity. Williams served two years until her post surgeon discovered her true identity. She was discharged with certificate of disability.

Eartha Kitt was conceived by rape on a plantation field that didn't stop what was meant to be she spoke five different languages and could sing in seven.

Know the story of June and Jennifer Gibbons?

Read this somewhere online "Every 28 days the cycle of the moon restores itself *the women and her cycle* the sun rises every morning *the man and his morning wood* LOL. The sun and the moon working together we are the Universe

Do you know Clara B. Williams story

Afro-Mexican (part of tribe of Juda) they were just recently a couple years ago in 2015 counted by the National Census they were discriminated against daily because of their darker skin tone.

Do you know who/what MONSANTO is? They have their hands in the Cannabis industry now.

Braids/Cornrolls were used by slave to relay messages and also for escape routes.

Ever heard of "The Atlanta Ripper"

Sergeant Henry Johnson also known as "The Black Death" kept Germans from crossing the line World War I killing a few and wounding a few more. He sustained a dozen plus wounds causing him to faint after the battle. After the war a parade was held to welcome them back home where he led the soldiers in. His discharge papers left his injuries out leaving him no disability check. Now go google him and see how his story ended.

Do you know what Chem Trail Lung is?

Amelia Bassano Lanier is behind some of Shakespeare's writings specially "Dark Lady" and maybe most of the others.

Wentworth Cheswell known as the very first African American judge in 1768 of New Hampshire was actually the right hand man of the known legend Paul Revere. You know the guy that yelled "The British are COMING!!" Well Revere wasn't the only one to take a ride that night. The reason we don't know about him is because Cheswell rode north while Revere rode west in lieu to seize Hancock and Adams and subsequently that's were all the action happened. All the people coming from up north Boston, Vermont and wherever else was because of Cheswell's ride.

Condoleezza Rice and Martin Luther King both started college at the age of 15 King attended Morehouse where he studied sociology and Rice attended University of Denver studying political science.

Have you ever looked into eating an organic raw vegan diet?

Familiar with Alice Ball and her contribution to leprosy?

OUR diets needs to be PLANT BASED greens fruits and WATER

Sam Cooke's questionable death came shortly after planning on helping X and King with their fight for liberation of the Black race with financial backing.

What is it in Liquor that can make you so extra aggressive and why are liquor stores so easy to find in the urban community.

Selma Hortense Burke a known American sculptor is the master mind which inspired the profile of Franklin D. Roosevelt on the dime.

So back in the day (slave days) when slaves planned on making a getaway they would not feed the blood hounds for a couple of days, when they finally made their run for it they would throw little snacks on the ground to distract the dogs. These snacks were cornmeal battered balls; yep you guessed it Hush Puppies.

Are you familiar with Selina Grey?

In 2005 a group of women from Kampala Uganda who work breaking rocks into gravel for the sum $1.20 a day decided that after donating to the victims of southeast Asia effected by the Tsunami and the help it did them it fell on their hearts again to give so a sum of two hundred workers came up with nine hundred in total to send over to the Katrina victims despite all they were asked to do was to pray.

Do you know what the ancient meaning of Diva or Thug is?

In some parts of Africa Albino body parts are believed to contain magic which lead to being attacked and their body parts sold on the black market, also in some parts being an Albino represents being cursed leading to discrimination or death so in 2016 Nairobi, Kenya held its own first ever in the World Albino Beauty Pageant to overcome this stigma

Did you know GMO's where placed in foods secretly since 1996?

Sophia Stewart is the author and original creator of The Terminator and The Matrix franchise after a six year dispute she won a two point five billion lawsuit for trademark violations. I really like Warner Bro's too SMH

Dathie Haines daughter of a Black man and mother who was Indian Cherokee making her the owner of 600 Acres of land. She was kidnapped in woods while picking berries. Sold as a personal slave and tricked into signing her land over.

Chicago was founded by Jean Baptiste Pointe Du Sable being the first permanent settler of Chicago in 1790. He was officially recognized as the founding father of Chicago in 1968.

Four years after retiring boxing Ali devoted himself self to humanitarian needs in 1990 he went to Iraq to persuade Saddam to release his fifteen American civilian hostages he held as his own personal shield. After about a week of being in Iraq interacting with Iraqis alike Saddam finally showed himself. After Ali assured him he would show America "An honest account" of Iraq. Saddam replied "I'm not going to let Muhammad Ali return to the U.S. without having a number of American citizens accompanying him." On Dec. 2, 1990 Ali and all fifteen hostages made it back home to the U.S.A.

Do you know what a "False Flag Attack" means?

Do you know who Krotoa A.K.A Eva was?

Matthew A. Cherry is ex-football player who turned movie director who has a Short Film called Hair Love about an African American father attempting to do his daughters hair.

August 25, 1967 it was said the FBI puts out internal order to disrupt ALL Black Liberation Groups

Book "How to Make Negro Christians" was written during slavery by a major slave owner Rev Dr. Charles Colcock Jones. He owned the plantations and developed a system to make slaves more submissive and easier to control by converting them to Christianity over time his methods proved successful and became standard operating system for handling slaves

Do you know what Apocrypha is?

In 1849 Henry "Box" Brown shipped himself to freedom from Virginia the Philadelphia's anti-slavery office in a three by two foot box and two feet eight inches deep for a twenty seven hour trip with "This side up" and "handle with care" written on the box. Leaving his wife and kids behind later bragging about how he did it and ruining any changes for other slaves to escape.

There is an Island called North Sentinel Island it is part of the Andaman Islands part of the Indian Union Territory. People here are known as Sentinelese and they desire to be left alone and untouched by today's modern world. In fact it's been known that they are known to react with violence to ward off visitors or voyagers, because they tend to reject contact with people outside their world they are isolated people or lost tribes who are untouched by modern day civilization. I would have to say these groups of people are what I consider "real" gangsters.

Did you know over fifty countries have banned or restricted labels of all GMO's?

Capital of republic of New Afrika was attacked on August 18, 1971 by police

Snow White was said to have been thought of or made up with Freddi Washington in mind keeping her "Imitation of Life" leading role in mind.

Alex Hayley born Alexander Murray Palmer "Alex" Haley August 11, 1921- February 10, 1992 Haley was a writer and author. You may know him form the book or ABC'S television series ROOTS. ROOTS was based off Haley's true ancestors he found through genealogical research while doing his 20 years in the coast guards. Well that was what I believed for a very long time. Alex Haley's "ROOTS" was a case of plagiarism where the original author Harold Courlander the author of "the African" sued Haley and won the case. After roots miniseries aired Genealogy became a huge public interest.

Did you know there was a Casual Killing Act back in 1669 if a slave died while disobeying their master the slave owner would not be punished? This act was actually made to protect the White woman whom was killing high volume of young Black children by beating them to death in attempt to correct them to do better.

Johnnie L. Cochran Jr. was about to work on getting Black People reparations before he died.

The original Black Friday meaning I've heard over the years Black Friday dates back all the way to when slavery was still in place. In my slight research I've come to find yes Black Friday is dated all the way back but not connected toward selling slaves the day after thanksgiving. It actually dates back to Philly when then had their football and basketball game day of course with a lot of shopping Some Philly police came up with the name black Friday hopping it would leave a bad taste in some people mouth and die down all the commotion and traffic. *I could be wrong but hey that's what I found*shoulder shrug**

James Cameron is the only known Surviving victim of a lynching attempt

George Junius Stinney Jr. is the youngest person to be executed. Stinney was sentenced at ten years of age after a ten min deliberation and electrocution at fourteen. He was buried in an unmarked grave by family in hopes he could rest in peace. After t decades plus his conviction was posthumously vacated and his execution ruled cruel and unusual punishment.

Lone Ranger was based off of one of the first Black deputy U.S. marshals west of Mississippi river, Bass Reeves. Reeves worked Oklahoma and Arkansas the most he captured more 3,000 criminals. Reeves was the first black deputy to serve along the west Mississippi River. He was the man I guess you could say he bought in some of the deadliest criminals, had to arrest his own son for murder, and was very valuable when it came to the Indian territories because he knew many of their languages. He worked a total of thirty five years and was never wounded on the job.

The hated yet most loved word out.
NGA Naga, Negash (Nigeria) = Queen
NGU Negu, Negus (Niger) = King
NGR NETERU, NTRU, (Netjer) = God
NTR Neter= Nature/Power/Energy
Nigger/Nigga= offensive term to describe a black or dark skinned person

So check this out I know that we hate when the opposite race refer to us as nigga or niggers or you see other race refer to their obvious not black friend as nigga and all in the name of love it disturbs you a little bit, it def tugs on something inside of me. But when you sit and think about it we really can't get mad. Don't get me wrong it is one of my biggest pet peeves. For me to hear any opposite race use it or even for a group of black folk to continuously use it loudly in mixed company. I only say this because when you really sit down and think about it it's displayed in everything that's tied to the black community you might listen to a R&B or rap song and you might hear the word Nigga you might Be watching your favorite movie and might hear the word Nigga you might be listing to your favorite celebrity of social media famous person page and they may refer to someone as…nigga. I don't even think it's censored on T.V. anymore I really don't know I can't watch the television without my head hurting…it's a waste! So at the end of the day since black culture is basically the epitome of America, the word is used so recklessly. The only way you change somebody from saying that and actually have them scared of using it is if you don't use it. If you take every bitch every nigga every negative word that you use to reach out to somebody in a so called lovable manner and you replace that with brother sister king and queen you'll have everybody out here so confused they wouldn't know what to do and they darn sure would be scared to say it at least in front of you and as they should, because they don't know how you are going to react. **If you want something to change if you want to have a right to something you really have to be an example.** Thoroughly you have to be an example and take those words out of you vocabulary and lead. It's definitely not just you it's also the people that you talk to get on them about it, speak to your favorite celeb in their comments speak to their conscious don't harass and troll just be the disappointed fan that comment they will see it, trust.

They are human and want a better future for the generation I'm sure at least half do and that's all you need to build a force. Believe it or not a lot of the things I talk about in this book they know probably been known but in the same sentence they probably believe you we aren't going to listen. Their thinking they don't want to hear that remember they are celebrities they have to do what they have to do in order to stay relevant. Voice your opinion just like that celeb voices theirs and get everybody on the bandwagon a couple of us can voice our opinions and encourage a celeb to hop on board. It's something we really need to change. But that's just my opinion.

Money is made out of cotton fiber paper not wood fiber like most paper. Picked so much cotton had to find something special to do with it I guess.

Were you aware vaccines contain mercury (thimerosal)

Did you know there is a Miss Black America Pageant? It debuted in September of 1977

Canada also recognizes black history in February while the UK also recognizes it also but in the month of October.

A tribe of Masai People of Kenya gave 14 cows to the U.S. towards the relief of 9/11. Cows are valued at a very high possession and considered highest expression of sympathy and regards.

Did you know some officers may raise their hoods to cover their dash cams?

Do you think if we get the Government to pay for our health care like England they would stop feeding us poison?

Massa: slave owners documented "Massa" was broken English from slaves who could not pronounce master. In Hebrew dialect Massa means burden or oppressor.

"The Ethel Waters Show" aired on June 14 1939 was the

Netta B.

first African American to star in her own show via television a special variety show.

The eve gene (mitochondrial DNA) this is such a big topic basically when I read over it I get that at the end of the day man derived in Africa and a lot of people do not want to hear that. I don't know where exactly I stand with the whole topic belief or disbelief I just really do find it extremely interesting at the end of the day.

Look up omnivore carnivore and herbivores intestine tracts and why it's built like that now compare to your intestines what do you think you should eat?

Have you ever really considered fasting from the media (television, internet, and radio)?

Banjo was made by Caribbean blacks in the 17 century

Where do our last names derive from? I always have this thing of where did my last name come from or who in my tree did what. So when you think about when whomever and however many of us came across the waters people were crossing over to their new destiny they didn't keep their first or last names slave owners gave them names that were easy for them themselves to pronounce and remember, like their very own last name. When slavery was abolished yes a few slaves disowned their slave owners names while others kept it not able to go back or maybe not even remember what their true identity was. Some adopted names that were associated with freedom or different patriots names like Jefferson, Washington, Freeman etc.

MELANIN

Do you know what the Raw Food Pyramid is?

Malcolm X has a day something I did not know until recently, it's not a federal holiday. Malcolm X Day is celebrated on May 19th his birthday or the third Sunday of May. A commemoration has been proposed as an official state holiday in the U.S. state of Illinois in 2015. Some other interesting info on Malcolm I came across he and a guy named Pio Gama Pinto made an alliance in the early 1960's they planned on going to the United Nations on behalf of the Black race to have the United States charged on human rights violations. In 1965 both men were assassinated four days apart from each other.

So the state California is named after a Black Amazon Warrior Queen Calafia?

Do you know who Dapper Dan is he helped create hip hop and its look he was the go to man for most rappers athlete singers anybody who was anybody or wanted to look like somebody in 80's early 90's. He owned a store in Harlem during the 1982 till 1992. Looks like Louis Vuitton used one of his earlier designs from years ago recently and may be looking to collaborate with him.

Alkaline water or drinking from copper cups so it's said to aide in weight-loss, a brain stimulant, slow down the aging process, anti-cancer, anti-inflammatory, and antimicrobial. I would consider it a homemade alkaline water to help with PH balance.
Do you know the benefits of alkaline water or copper cups/mugs/vessels and green vegetables alone?
Our past ancestors used to drink out of them the Kings and Queens

Wonder Woman is based off of the superheroine Nubia who was an Amazon her character was created in 1973 she had over ten special abilities like fly, paralyze, super strong but the best one is she could heal her body of injury by becoming one with the earth soil and reforming herself. Her recent character named Nu'Bia was created and first appeared in 1999.

I always wonder why is Vanilla is white washed lol comes in a brown bean and as a brown substance that's always been weird to me. Did you know Edmund Albius helped start the sweet vanilla industry?

Sarah Bartman born Saartjie Baartman 1789-December 29 1815 was known as Hottentot Venus she displayed as a freak show attraction in the 19th century in Europe. She traveled to England with an employer a free black that had in mind solely for money. She spent four years on stage doing acts which some saw to be inappropriate and thought she had been doing so against her will. A trail took placed that proved documents of a contract and the courts ruled in favor of her continued exhibition. Bartman was sold to an animal trainer where she continued her human zoo show. In 1815 after Bartman death her body was dissected and her remains were put on display to view at the Museum of Man in Paris for over a century. In 2002 her remains were returned to Africa and she was buried in Eastern Cape she died of an unknown inflammatory disease.

Diddy open up prep school "Capital Prep Harlem School" in 2016, that's what I'm talking build a whole school for a community.

Body organs on the black market organ harvesting black woman and girls missing, Melanin sells for 384.50 . A lot of people believe the movie "Get Out" is a hinting towards the reality of Human organ trafficking or Black Organ Harvesting in the black market. I believe if Organ Donor is on your driver's license you should reconsider and maybe take it off. Once you pass away your Organ now belong to the government, and you never know you may need those organs in order to tell what really what happened or what was going on or happening to your body before you died. Do you know the story of Kendrick Johnson I find his story so strange, things that make you go umm.

Look up Black Organ Harvesting

If it's seedless it's probably fake

TWA People originally from Africa but migrated to Ireland over 10,000 years ago Where the leprechaun folk tale derived from. Saint Patrick is known for removing the snakes from Northern Ireland first of all it's too cold for snakes in Ireland and I believe the snakes they were referring to was a head garment that a pygmy African tribe wore. I said that since this tribe couldn't be forced into change or submission they were killed or ran away from the property. The whole leprechaun image comes from them being shorter and the pot of gold I would say refers to their land taken. It's like you celebrating your own genocide.

Memorial Day known then as Decorations Day in black history 1865 former black slaves started Memorial Day in

1865 in Charleston South Carolina almost three hundred dead Union Soldiers were buried in a mass grave at a confederate prison camp. After World War I it was recognized for all men and women who died in war or military action. June 28, 1968 Congress passed the Uniform Monday Holiday Act changing Memorial Day from May 30th to the last Monday in May.

Some say hurricanes are our ancestors form of payback for the era of Kidnapping, killing, and determent of Black people. It's known that a Hurricane is by far the most lethal and powerful form of a natural disaster they can last for a week with speeds higher than two hundred miles an hour. The thing that gets me is they only form on the northern and southwestern boarders of Africa taking the same routes of the slave trade middle passage.

Do you know why people say Black people are economically behind as a race? An article I stumbled on stated this, one being the one that made me say well duh!! **The only thing we know is consumption and don't understand the importance of building wealth.** With that being said why we want to flex on our brother or sister so bad majority of us are broke whether financially, mentally, or emotional wise. In order to get back ahead we must UNITE. The ideal course of habit we should be taking is keeping our coins within our community build Black, hire Black, buy Black, and spend Black. Can we get another Greenwood community?

The Roman Empire has had a prominent amount of black leaders. Black images still prevail in the European history.

What's the first Black recorded birth on record for the States? St Augustine, Florida In 1606 according to African American registry the name is William Tucker

The Talented Tenth term was designated to an African American class of leaders in the early twentieth century. The term was publicized by W.E.B. Du Bois in September of 1903 as an essay that appeared in "The Negro Problem" a collection of essays with the concept of in mind. **To describe the likelihood of one in every ten men would become leaders of their race in the world.**

The African American Holiday Association (AAHA) Yes if want to know what's going on in your world of color go check out the AAHA been in in practice since 1982 but incorporated in 1989 it's a none profit, member organization based out of D.C. Founded by Ayo Handy Kendi. They have expos, programs, classes, presentations, and youth services. Here are some holidays AAHA believes we should recognize

Black Love Day (BLD): is February 13th started in 1993
Unity and Diversity Day: is May 1 started in 1995
Ancestor Honor Day: is May 1st started in 1995
Kwanzaa: is Dec. 26 – Jan.1
Juneteenth: is June 19 day commemorates June 19th 1865 announcement of abolition of slavery
D.C. Emancipation Day: is April 16th this day in 1862 abolition of slavery in District of Columbia
Harriet Tubman Day: March 10th started in 1990
Women History Month: Month of March, Women's Week is week of March 8th which is Women's Day
Native American History Month: Month of November started in 1990

Grandmothers Day: First Sunday after Labor Day started in 1978
National Black AIDS Awareness Day: Feb. 7th
World Aids Day: is Dec. 1st started in 1988 (**National HIV Testing Day** June 27th started in 1995) go get a free test this day.
World Asthma Day/Month: First Tuesday in May started in 1998
International Breath Day: ??
Mandela Day: is July 18th started in 2010
Black Marriage Day: not sure what day it falls on or how its placed but the month seems to be March or April I'm guessing whatever state you are in over 30,000 communities participate in this event conducting events, presentations, couples counseling, and marriage retreats. This event started back in 2003
Indigenous Peoples' Day: On October 9, 2017 some people recognized Columbus Day as Indigenous Day in salute to the American Indian Nation that was already here long before Columbus set sail.

The MOVE 9

Debbie Sims Africa #006307; Janet Hollaway Africa #006308; Janine Phillips Africa #006309 451 Fullerton Ave. Cambridge Springs, PA 16403-1238
Delbert Orr Africa #AM 4985 1000 Follies Rd. Dallas, PA 18612
Michael Davis Africa #AM 4973; Charles Sims Africa #AM 4975 P.O. Box 244 Graterford, PA 19426-0246
Edward Goodman Africa #AM 4974 301 Morea Rd. Frackville, PA. 17932
Merle Africa passed away on March 13, 1998
William Phillips Africa passed Jan. 2015

They have a petition for their release floating around.

Have you ever heard of the term Geoengineering?

Betty Boop Baby Esther born Esther Jones not sure when she was born but she died in 1934. Esther was the singing style and appearance that originated Betty Boop Helen Kane was simply the voice. To learn more check out the Kane v. Fleischer case.

Money with black faces on it
Marcus Garvey is on Jamaican Currency
Numista Gregory 3rd of England is on a half penny
General Hannibal AKA Hannibal Barca Triumph coin of Hannibal 203 B.C

KIND OF A HOT COMMODITY
Coins from island of Lesbos circa 500-550 B.C.
Barbados coppers 1788-1792
(Do you have any?)

225TH ANNIVERSARY Coin
In April 2017 a 24 karat gold coin was issued with a "black" Lady liberty (product code17XA)

Are you familiar with the chemical Astrazine or Tyrone Hayes?

Drugs
I got to talk about drugs I was a D.A.R.E kid

So try and vibe with me for a second on this drug thing

so when your peers say I'm getting this money hustling independent or for self, yes in a sense this is true but when you selling throwing shit around for someone else getting fronted you lying because you working for someone you are not independent that shit was brought and will continue to be brought by "some unknown source" maybe by the say person or linage of that person who wanted to run us back in the day that entrepreneur that business man who owned the plantation, the man that owed the farm the banks whatever, I believe that who is running that and got you running in circles. You can come up but do you ever really leave or break ties? No you implement more problems for yourself bigger maybe even personal problems. You thinking, planning, even trusting in people you don't even truly know it's a gamble you not in shit alone nor independently. Just look at these people I've mentioned they are recognized from decades and centuries ago from the betterment not determent of their doings. People got on and by being true to self they went after their goal dreams and what they believe their calling was and that's how they got on. Just really think about it, drugs are geared and placed in our communities it serves a purpose to both the user and entrepreneur. One forgets its pain and quiets giving into self-pity while the other feeds off its pain and stores the self-pity as fuel. Either way it takes away from our community both parties are intelligent people party A is using his energy towards the wrong thing and party B has just given up on using its energy most of the users I know are smart really intelligent could teach you something, remember everything, and build a whole house electric and all but just reached a ultimate breaking point mentally. Its implemented and placed to stop us destroy and concourse specifically for us and it just so happed to

MELANIN

evolve

Taking gifts and blessing from both parties

"I believe unconditionally in the ability of people to respond when they are told the truth. We need to be taught to study rather than believe, to inquire rather than to affirm."

Septima Poinsette Clark

Netta B.

NOTES

Netta B.

THIS IS SO COOL TO ME

Ok You probably wondering this girl got up her sleeve now, what she bout to write about now? This here section is something different. You know how somebody is always in Africa digging or "finding" something? Well that's always made me feel like what is it, what's over there why they just don't go to some of these big "cool" states and dig something up? They love going over to this "poor" country and take away. That's when I knew something was special about Africa that it is truly rich continent and when I say rich I mean in many ways from culture, land, and history. A few things stick out to me as far as mainly the culture was brought over here from holidays to religion to whatever else you want to name and Europeans put a spin on it to fit or entertain themselves. I'm not trying to force any opinions onto anyone we deal with that daily I'm just here to maybe open up the eye just a little bit more. These things are of African culture.

Medusa was an African serpent goddess who carried live snakes in a pouch around her waist that represented wisdom and renewal. Her name represents wisdom while she represented truth, and her on her head were dreadlocks. Europeans who seen nothing like her made up her hair being snakes not understanding or knowing of dreads saying her head bore snakes because of the snakes she carried and said she would turn any man into stone because of the Gorgon mask she carried that was painted red with fanged teeth a protruding tongue and glaring eyes to frighten off the unskilled.

I wonder if Lucy (AL 288-1) is really just a monkey of is she the Queen that started it all. Look, my mind it doesn't quit. Lol

Black cats were not always bad luck. Goddess Bastet was a black cat known for keeping evil spirits away.

Slaves fled over to Africa on 70AD from romans so they wouldn't be used as servants or slaves. It's said that Africans Hamites sold the Israelites to the slave ships that is why black people that are in America from a long line of lineage that connects to ancestors being in slavery. Some say mainly Africans say we are not African but American. Or they may say "at least my ancestors were smart enough not to get caught." It's because mainly Israelites and "few" Africans were brought back to the states. Most blacks in America are not descendants of African but Hebrew Israelites, Tribe of Judah /children of Israel or maybe your ancestors were already here and you really have Indian all through you. 1619 is when slavery started Israelites being captive and held captive taken from the western coast of Africa. Slaves were sent to Jamestown and sold as bonds men and bonds women while a few of the colored people that were already here may have been tricked into slavery.

Nubians are believed to be one of the earliest Cradles of Civilization.

Did you know Vatican's and Popes worship the original image of Virgin Mary and Jesus Christ which are the black Madonna and Yahshua. Europeans for some reason have a lot of the original and true images throughout their country

Ever heard of Saint Maurice leader of legendary Roman Theban Legion

Taharqa ruler of Naoatan Kush from 690-664 B.C a Nubian King at the age of sixteen

Oldest university founded was found in Africa university of Al-Karaouine founded 859 AD Fez Morocco Africans studied the universe / astronomy = university

Priest/doctors date back to 1600 BC even cannabis was mentioned in medical treatments. Doctors, Mid-wives, Dentists came around Imhotep time. There is a lot of evidence from the remains of mummies and other remains of proof of successful surgery and amputations. Prosthetic limbs even surgical instruments have been found like probes, bandages, catheter, scalpel, sponges, forceps, bone saw, etc. and mostly all medicines were taken internally. They even believed in a changed diet and healthy way of eating to be important to health. Another pretty cool thing back around 1600 B.C. is how women took their pregnancy text which was to urinate on seeds barley and wheat. After a few days of waiting verses our few minutes if the barley sprouted they expected a boy if the wheat blossomed they expected a girl if neither grew no one was pregnant. Men were never present during birth always the pregnant and four other females be it family midwives or whomever

Ancient Africans studied the stars, sun, and moon for over fifty thousand years creating the 365 day calendar. Have you ever heard of the Lebombo bone?

Gold teeth diamond/ gems in teeth just looking thru the internet could not find too much on gold grillz and how they relate to our ancestors. But it is apparent that Egyptians were very familiar with the human body due to mummification they had to drain the body and whatever else which gave them a visual and understanding of the human body. They had a clear understanding because how else could you drill teeth without hitting pulp and form medicines for the pain. A new wave is starting back up where people are getting tooth gems or tooth bling again.

Ankh the Egyptian cross is a symbol of eternal life, the key of life, cross of life, joy of life, and energy. It is known as the original cross, created by Africans in Ancient Egypt and carried by the Egyptian Gods by its handle or in both hands with arms crossed over chest. Associated with water it also symbolize conception and believed to regenerating life, sun, air, and the Gods who carried it.

Is it a coincidence the Ankh and Female Sex Symbol look so much alike?

Yoga which means Union originated in Africa but Africans and Indian practices going back about five thousand years ago learning and mastering the "Mystery System"

So someone once asked me why I don't really get excited about holidays and it's just that they want us extinct. Don't you realize every holiday we celebrate has a mythical background, story from Africa, or an evil and disturbing beginning? Have you ever looked up or searched "Pagan Holidays" or any holiday for that matter?
So you telling me every holiday that come by I have to spend hundreds dollars just to celebrate and enjoy a season I have to buy people gifts to show I care or thought about them? You know how many people I know? You know how much money that is? I have never really given gifts on holidays. In my eyes holidays are just overtime money days for the government it's all about money I'm not celebrating. The real holidays are people birthday's and maybe deaths days that you really celebrate them or enjoy them that's a celebration. But other holidays like Easter, Halloween hate to say it but Christmas what do we really know what is this that we are celebrating something that started years ago and we don't even know what is what how can one event one thing have so many stories a thousand versions? It's all about thinking doing for self not to fit in or conform we conform enough with jobs and taxes now your being told how to spend certain days in a year and it's a repeat for next year too? Naw I'm good. What do you really believe

or know and what are you disagreeing or agreeing with? Holidays.

GOD IS WITHIN YOU BECAUSE YOU ARE AN IMAGE OF HIM

Is it AMEN or AMEN-RA?

The Original Holy Trinity

The Original Holy Trinity story goes like this. It is Ausar (male), Aset (female), and Heru (child) Asuar was murdered by his brother who cut his body into pieces and scattered them throughout the city. Aset his newly wife is devastated and sad because they had yet to consummate their marriage, so she goes and retrieves every body part she could find retrieving all but his penis resurrecting him from the dead. Both wanted to make love and create a child that Aset turned herself into a bird hovering over Asur becoming pregnant and being the true Virgin Mary.
Kemet/Ancient KMT was the original name for Egypt it meant Black lands or black soil. Kemetic was more so a way of life then following scripture. Every African Society had their African spirituality base but all observed the Principles of MA'AT.

7 principles of Kemet
1. There is but one Universal Order
2. There is one Cosmic Unity
3. There is only one measure
4. There is one cosmic law that precedes all spiritual

laws
5. There is only one intelligence
6. There is only one path
7. There is only one reality

Maat have you ever heard of Maat THE Goddess of Truth and Justice? Maat or Ma'at represents or has seven cardinal principles which are justices, balance, harmony, order, truth, righteous, and propriety, known to be the ancient Egyptian concepts. These rules or laws was to avert chaos and it was the basis of Egyptian law to represent the moral and ethical principles every Egyptian was expected to follow throughout daily life involving self, family, a community, the nation, to god and the environment.

7 Codes/Laws of Maa
1. Maa is Truth and is based upon perspective
2. Maa is Balance and is limited by the mind
3. Maa is Harmony and becomes what attention is focused on
4. Maa is Justices and doing what is right, right now.
5. Maa is Love and Love is Exchange
6. Maa is Order and not coincidence
7. Maa is Propriety and doing what is relevant

"Ma'at is good and its worth is lasting. It has not been disturbed since the day of its creator, whereas he who transgresses its ordinance is punished. It lies as a path in front even of him who knows nothing. Wrong doing has never yet bought its venture to port. It is true that evil may gain wealth but the strength of truth is that it lasts: a man can say: "It was the property of my father.""

~Instruction of Ptahhotep~

42 Declarations

1. I have not committed sin.
2. I have not committed robbery with violence
3. I have not stolen.
4. I have not slain men and women.
5. I have not stolen grain.
6. I have not purloined offerings.
7. I have not stolen the property of the gods.
8. I have not uttered lies.
9. I have not carried away food
10. I have not uttered curses.
11. I have not committed adultery.
12. I have made none to weep.
13. I have not eaten the heart
14. I have not attacked any man
15. Iam not a man of deceit
16. I have not stolen cultivated land
17. I have not been a esdropper
18. I have not slandered
19. I have not been angry without just cause
20. I have no debauched the wife of any man
21. I have not debauched the wife of any man
22. I have not polluted myself
23. I have terrorized none
24. I have not transgressed.
25. I have not been wroth.
26. I have not shut my ears to the words of truth
27. I have not blasphemed.
28. Iam not a man of violence.
29. I am not a stirrer up of strife
30. I have not acted with undue haste.
31. I have not pried into matters

32. I have not multiplied my words in speaking.
33. I have wronged none, I have done no evil.
34. I have not worked witchcraft against the king.
35. I have never stopped water.
36. I have never raised my voice.
37. I have not cursed God.
38. I have not acted with evil rage.
39. I have not stolen the bread of the gods.
40. I have not carried away the Khenfu cakes from the spirits of the dead.
41. I have not snatched away the bread of the child, nor treated with contempt the God of my city.
42. I have not slain the cattle belonging to the God.

These deities have been recorded in history as far back as twenty three hundred years ago. These laws actually remind me of the Ten Commandments.

"There is no yesterday for the lazy person, no friend for the one who is deaf to Maat, no festival day for the greedy."

Ma'at The eleven Laws of God

1. Law of Amen (you were created in the likeliness of a peace which cannot be disturbed. Regain your original state of peace to attain to your reason for coming into existence the enjoyment of life.
2. Law of Ausar (your nature is a unconquerable peace. Therefore, nothing and no one in the world can be against you. All experience come to you to promote your reclamation of peace, that you may turn acquire wisdom and spiritual power.
3. Law of Tehuti (When your thoughts, feelings and

actions reflect the word of god, then the power of gods spirit and a peace that nothing can challenge will flow through your being.

4. Law of Sekher (when the emotions of man manifest in response to the word of the God they have the power to influence any and all events in the world.
5. Law of Ma'at (God needs you in order to come into the world. Fulfilling gods need is the highest act of love and only through your love for God can you fulfill your love for others. Become Gods love in the world for the protection of the world
6. Law of Herukhutt (know that God neither punishes nor rewards nor protects. You will have the comforts of controlling these for yourself.
7. Law of Heru (You have the power but not the right to ignore Gods law. Choose to follow gods law with love and joy that comes from understanding and the wisdom and power of gods spirit will flow through your being.
8. Law of Het-Heru (it is not what you imagine but who is imagining. Are you a human or a divine being?
9. Law of Sebek (It is not what you think or affirm. It is who is thinking or affirming. Are you a human or divine being.
10. Law of Auset (Prepare ro sacrifice everything to become the vessel of God on earth and you will, in turn, receive everything.
11. Law of Geb (know that from heaven you came and to heaven you will return, seek not enduring works on earth

Kente cloth made of silk, cotton, and/or rayon all patterns have its own names and meanings Kente cloth was invented by two Akan men in 1690.

How big is Africa? 11.73 million miles and the world's second largest continent. Covers 6 percent of the earth surface and 20.4 percent of its total land area it has a population of 1.216 billion reported as of 2016.

What is Black?

Adjective- of the very darkest color owning to the absence of or complete absorption of light; the opposite of white. Of any human group having dark-colored skin, especially of African or Australian Aboriginal ancestry.

Noun- black color or pigment. A member of a dark-skinned people, especially one of African or Australian aboriginal ancestry.

Verb- make black

Merriam-Webster: 1.the color of coal, the opposite of white 2. Black clothing He is dressed in black 3. A person belonging to a race of people having dark skin 4. An American having black African ancestors: African Americans.

What is a Black Man?

A person with dark skin who comes from Africa or whose ancestors come from Africa.
What is known to be black decent? History has it as Australia, Andaman Island, India, Pacific Islands, Malaysia. Russia, china, and Africa

I'm not saying everything I presented in this chapter to be God send the gospel I'm just saying that I'm opened minded and eyes wide a lot that is present has been presented has the potential to be. I'm just saying isn't it possible, why couldn't a certain hated, disliked, beautiful smart race encourage a nation? I mean can a person who hates water put a pinch or squirt of something in it to make it better in their eyes then entice a friend to try and love it? Yes and that person invented Kool-Aid. LOL. I'm just saying its food for thought. Just because it's written in stone with pictures to match doesn't make it true, how does it add up?

I'm not saying we all came from Africa I'm just saying we are the original people personally I believe my roots all stem from American soil I think I'm owned some land verse reparations LOL.

> *"Love is man's natural endowment but he doesn't know how to use it. He refuses to recognize the power of love because of his love of power."*
>
> *Dick Gregory*

MELANIN

Netta B.

NOTES

A FEW PLACES TO VISIT

In this chapter Places to see is something big because how many of us in reality know about the museums historic site or whatever that's in our very own the city we are born or even raised in? Our own stomping grounds can sometimes be very foreign to some because they follow a certain routine or just not exposed to doing more than school work home or family and friends. There are multiple historic landmarks and museums in the United States that honors our Ancestors. I believe it's important to just take your child, brother, sister, cousin whatever, one time in their life I'm sure it will be something that leaves a mark on them and how they see things. On vacations or even in your own home town go out and explore learn some history it may not be advertised but a couple key words can pull it right up in your search engine.
If you're not into going and getting on the internet and

researching some of the things that I have presented in the book so far then that's the good thing about this chapter. Reading and experiencing is great because you have your mind going and things happing in the brain which is good. So yeah going into a museum and actually reading and seeing the picture or memorabilia will mean something more for all the hands on people like myself. This chapter can lead you to the person you seen in this book that you actually grew a liking to they may have a full museum about them and their legacy. There are so many museums in the world and throughout the states. Because most museums aren't advertised there are a lot of people that are oblivious and blind to the fact of what kind of culture a city even their city can hold, a true hidden treasure.

Niagara Falls Underground Railroad Heritage area- **Niagara Falls, New York**

Freedom statue on Goree Island, The House of Slaves, Door of no Return museum and memorial to the Atlantic slave trade. Located off the coast of **Dakar Senegal** it is said to represent the final exit point of the slaves from Africa

National Museum of African American History and Culture- **Washington, D.C. National Mall**

African American museum-**Cleveland, Ohio**

Fort Lyon- **Bent County, Colorado**

Pyramid of Djoser- **Saqqara, Egypt**

Central Pennsylvania African American Museum- **Reading, Pennsylvania**

National Museum of African Art- **Washington, D.C. National Mall**

Colonel Allensworth State Historic Park- **Allensworth, California**

Wells Built Museum- **Orlando, FL**

Anacostia Community Museum- **Washington, D.C. Anacostia**

The International Afro American Museum also known as Charles H. Wright Museum of African American History- **Detroit, Mich.**

National Voting Rights Museum-**Selma, Alabama**

The Bridget "Biddy" Mason Monument- **Los Angeles, California**

America Black Holocaust Museum-**Milwaukee Wisconsin**
reopened as a **Virtual Museum** in 2012

Aburi Botanical Gardens there is a tree Family tree of Africans all over the world carved tree powerful image in Aburi Gardens located in **Aburi in South Ghana**

Freedmen Cemetery also known as Contrabands and Freedmen Cemetery basically during the American Civil War Alexandria transformed into a Union controlled area under complete ARMY control which meant slaves could escape to Alexandria and gain something like freedom by fighting in the war. Now because these people fleeing were still legally slaves and owned by someone they were labeled contrabands to be prevented from being returned to their owners. Some that made to Alexandria didn't come in the best health and may have died due to poor living conditions and sickness in the air. So a cemetery was drawn and made up specifically for them. *Which is where possibly the name comes from.*

Underground Railroad Heritage Trail- **Rochester, New York**

Old Courthouse (Jefferson National Expansion Memorial) - **St. Louis, Missouri**

Public Schools of Washington D.C. - **District of Columbia**

Brown v. Board of Education National Historic Site- **Topeka, Kansas**

Valley of the Kings- **Egypt**

Valley of the Queens- **Egypt**

Nicodemus National Historic Site- **Nicodemus, Kansas**

Hitsville U.S.A. Motown historical museum the start of

Motown records and home of owner Barry Gordy located in **Detroit, Michigan**

Bass Reeves Statue-**Fort Smith, Arkansas**

Slave Mart Museum- **Charleston South, Carolina**

James H. Dillard Home- **New Orleans, Louisiana**

African American Hall of Fame- **Peoria, Illinois**

Black Panther Tours- **Oakland, California**

National Civil Rights Museum- **Memphis, Tennessee**

Boston African American National Historic Site- **Boston, Massachusetts**

Temple of Hatshepsut- **Luxor, Kemet**

Underwater sculpture in Grenada also known as Molinere Underwater Sculpture Park is located in the **Caribbean Sea West Coast of Grenada**. The creator has six galleries under sea each being installed in a two year span. There is one called Vicissitudes where 26 kids are holding hands in a circle facing outwards has this speculation about it representing the slaves thrown overboard from slave ships during the African holocaust then there is another stating it represents life's ongoing cycle and the importance of creating sustainable and well managed environment for the youth. Either meaning they both get my vote. And the sculpture is beautiful.

Fort Pillow State Park- **Fort Pillow, Tennessee**

Clearview Golf Club- **East Canton, Ohio**

A Philip Randolph Pullman Porter Museum- **Chicago**

The National Great Black Wax Museum- **Baltimore, MD**

Howard High School considered to be one of the first black secondary schools in the nation is linked with the decision in the Brown v. Board of Education it was the first school to offer full high school curriculum to Black students- **Willington, Delaware**

The Egyptian Pyramids – **Egypt**

National Center of Afro-American Artist- **Roxbury, Massachusetts**

Mosaic Templars Cultural Center- **Little Rock, Arkansas**

Cape Coast Castle/Gate of no Return located in **Cape Coast, Ghana**

the break through the mold at String therapy high in **Philly**

Harvey B. Grantt Center for African American Arts and Culture-**Charlotte, North Carolina**

Egyptian Museum- **Cairo, Egypt**

The Martin Luther King Historic District- **Atlanta Ga.**

Frederick Douglas National Historic Site- **Washington D.C.**

Elmina Castle/Elmina slave dungeon located in **Elmina Castle**

Northwest African American Museum- **Seattle, Washington**

Freedmens Town end of civil wars freedmen purchase and land and built homes up the Buffalo Bayou because of the growth of schools, stores, churches, jazz clubs and theaters it was names "Little Harlem' it flourished for over six decades. During the great depression it deteriorated in 1984 it became a historic district.

Ashton Villa- **Galveston, Texas**

Lincolnville Historic District- **St. Augustine, Florida**

Austin F. Williams Carriage house was a station on the Underground Railroad and served as living quarters for the Amistad Africans on their way back to Africa- **Farmington, Connecticut**

Obelisk- **Replicas of this are all over the world**

Great Blacks in Wax Museum- **Baltimore, Maryland**

Tuxteco Museum- **Veracruz Mexico**

MELANIN

Great Sphinx of Giza- **Egypt**

Old Dillard Museum- **Fort Lauderdale, Florida**

The Hollywood Walk of Fame- **Hollywood, California**

Harriet Tubman Underground Railroad Visitor Center- **Church Creek, Maryland**

African American Firefighter Museum- **Los Angeles, California**

W.E.B. Du Bois Institute for African and African American Research- **Harvard University in Cambridge, Massachusetts**

New Philadelphia was one of the first towns registered by a Freedmen Frank McWhorter. He bought his and his family freedom along with an estimated 40 acres of land in Illinois. His town was a safe haven for the Underground Railroad. Today it is only an open field named a national landmark in 2009.

Rutherford B.H. Yates House- **Houston, Texas**

Ossian Sweet House- **Detroit, Michigan**

Kingsley Plantation Oldest plantation known in Florida now a house museum- **Jacksonville, Florida**

Daisy Bates House was a home that was a safe haven to the nine black children desegregating Little Rock Central

Netta B.

High in 1957- **Little Rock, Arkansas**

Mortuary Temple of Hatshepsut- **Egypt**

Mary McLeod Bethune Council House National Historic Site- **Washington, D.C**

International Civil Rights Center and Museum- **Greensboro, North Carolina**

Royall House and Slave Quarters- **Medford, Massachusetts**

Evergreen Plantation- **Wallace, Louisiana**

DuSable Museum of African American History- **Chicago, Illinois**

Mayme Agnew Clayton Western States Black Research and Education Center, Mayme A Clayton Library and Museum. Over a course of forty five years librarian Mayme Clayton collected 30,000 rare and out of print books located in **Culver City, California**

George Washington Carver Museum and Cultural Center this landmark is known for its Juneteenth exhibit- **Austin, Texas**

Overton Hygienic Building- **Chicago, Illinois**

Buffalo Soldiers Memorial Park- **Fort Leavenworth, Kansas**

Legacy Museum of African American History- **Lynchburg, Virginia**

Freedom Rides Museum- **Montgomery, Alabama**

Uncle Tom's Cabin Historic Site- **Dresden, Canada**

Pyramid of Teti- **Saqqara Egypt**

Tuskegee Airmen National Historic site- **Tuskegee, Alabama**

Jim Crow Virtual Museum- **Big Rapids, Michigan**

River Road African American Museum- **Donaldsonville, Louisiana**

National Underground Railroad Freedom Center is a museum paying homage to the Underground Railroad explaining the struggles of freedom back in the day while also looking at today and what could possibly be our future struggles; its center also focuses on human trafficking. Located in **Cincinnati, Ohio**

Martin Luther King Jr. National Historic Site- **Atlanta, Ga**

Luxor Temple- **Luxor, Egypt**

United States National Slavery Museum- **Fredericksburg, VA**

Sphinx- **Egypt**

New Orleans African American Museum of Art, Culture and History- **New Orleans, Louisiana**

August Wilson Center for African American Culture- **Pittsburgh, Pennsylvania**

Uncle Tom's Cabin the house Josiah Henson who is the supposed muse for the book is a historic site- **North Bethesda, Maryland**

Afro-American Historical and Cultural Society Museum- **Jersey City, New Jersey**

African American Civil War Memorial- **Washington D.C.**

Freedmens Town National Historic District- **Houston, Texas**

African American History Monument is the first monument made and dedicated to African Americans and the contributions to the State- **Columbia, South Carolina**

Brown v, Board of Education National Historic Site- **Topeka, Kansas**

African American Museum in Philadelphia this museum houses four galleries and an auditorium available with over 750,000 pieces of memorabilia available for loans to other facilities and research. They have temporary exhibits, family events and educational programs-

MELANIN

Philadelphia, Pennsylvania

Carter Plantation- **Springfield, Louisiana**

African-American Mosaic Exhibition- **Washington, D.C**

Harriet Tubman Underground Railroad National Monument- **Cambridge, Maryland**

Bunker Hill Monument- **Boston, Massachusetts**

Studio Museum in Harlem was the first African American fine arts devoted museum circa 1968 **College Museum was the first African American museum in Hampton Virginia in 1868**

I wonder what's in the Vatican City archives

"Racism is still with us. But it is up to us to prepare our children for what they have to meet, and hopefully, we shall overcome"

Rosa Parks.

Netta B.

THINGS YOU SHOULD KNOW BEING A AMERICAN U.S. CITIZEN

Ok so now-a-days everyone walks around screaming "I'm free" "I have rights" and don't even understand or know where to find these rights or how or when they received them or how and when to use them. So this section is just a quick reference guide so we can make sure you know what you're talking about. Learn the laws at least know what your ancestors were doing marches and sit-ins for, know the civil act rights. Now the national anthem it may or may not have some truths to it but maybe it could be a million dollar question, you need to know your surroundings you need to know and understand where you live, your country.

Now I believe all citizens should know the below things but this is mainly written for the purpose for you see what your race was fighting for and what was trying to be obtained as far as equality and justice verses what was going on to specific race and sex gender it was more so racial equality but also for people or a person as whole. Just imagine how many times something happened daily to make a black person not feel equal or inferior to white people. Each time those things happened there was no due process just guilty.

In my eyes it like you know how something is right there it's obtainable, it's there you can see it but you have to do something more than just grab it there is a slight reach, you have to hop, jump, stand on the tip of your toes. It's just something, one thing more you're going to have to do to just grasp it. That's basically why they were fighting

they seen it, the bigger and better picture and they were close to it. Their eyes seen people breaking, changing, they felt all the hostility and hate from others but seen and lived that and still continued to protest fight or challenge whatever their belief was at that time.
Yea states ran differently but at the end of the day our privilege was basically the same, extremely limited. You just have to imagine how hard it could be when this race hate wasn't even an issue it was just life. Someone so nasty and hateful to your race and not even for a reason just because of a color which is not a reason it's just the color of your skin. You move your skin and put theirs then what? Will you be different? Not at all same brain, mindset, walk voice and they wouldn't even know. This is the picture that all our greats seen, equality.

Emancipation Proclamation:
Presidential proclamation and executive order issued by President Abraham Lincoln January 1 1863. Although it was set to make slave free or freedmen this did not out law slavery or grant citizenship to ex-slaves. It was only for states in rebellion and did not apply to states like Kentucky Maryland Delaware Missouri or Tennessee, although if you escaped and got to the union lines you could see freedom.

Juneteenth
Is a celebration of when the news that slavery had ended General Gordan Granger and the Union soldiers he led passed the news the war was over and slaves were free. It can be celebrated in a day weekend, week, or month's celebration. The day or celebration period is usually filled with, song and dance, barbeques, picnics, music, guest speakers, history lessons, the commerate of freedom,

education, and achievements.

Civil Rights Act

There have been eight major Federal Laws known as Civil Rights Acts.

The most famous **Civil Rights Act of 1964** the landmark of **US Labor Laws** and civil rights in the United States that outlaws discrimination based on race, color, religion, sex, or nationality I public places, with education, employment, for everything. It's kind of the law for Equal Opportunity.

Civil Rights Act of 1965 or better known as the **Voting Rights Act of 1965** this prohibits racial discrimination in voting.

1866 law was passed by congress on the 9th of April 1866 over the veto of president Andrew Johnson IN 1865. The act stated all persons born in the United States were now citizens without regard to race color or previous condition. Same rights enjoyed by white citizens were extended to all male persons in the **US 1866 Civil Rights Act**

Civil Rights Act of 1871 also known as the **Force Act of 1871** or the Ku Klux Klan Act. This act empowered the president to suspend the right of habeas corpus. This act completely dismantled the first era of Ku Klux Klan organization.

The **Civil Rights Act of 1875** guarantees African Americans equal treatment in public accommodations and public transportations while also prohibiting exclusion from jury service.

Civil Rights Act 1957 ensures the right of all Americans the ability to vote.

1968 Civil Rights Act also known as the **Fair Housing Act** signed by Lyndon B. Johnson provided equal housing opportunities regardless of race color religion sex disability familial status or national origin the act also included the Indian bill of rights which extended protections to Native Americans.

Last but not least the **Civil Rights Act of 1991**, which is a labor law that gives you right to sue an employer for discrimination and right to trial.

Browder v Gayle case that desegregated buses in Montgomery, Plessy v. Ferguson supported racial segregation laws under the doctrine "separate but equal", and Brown v. Board of Education case found segregated schools were inherently unequal were some cases that helped during the reconstruction era.

The *Reconstruction* Amendments

The **Thirteenth Fourteenth and Fifteenth Amendments** all passed between 1865-1870 five years following the civil war. The three are sometime referred to as the civil war amendments. It had been sixty one years since an amendment had been added to the first twelve amendments some may call it a **Reconstruction Era**.

The Thirteenth Amendment abolished slavery and involuntary servitude except as punishment for a crime (December 6, 1865)

The Fourteenth Amendment addresses citizenship rights and equal protection of the laws for all persons. (July 9, 1868)

The Fifteenth Amendment prohibits discrimination in voting rights of citizens on the basis of race, color, or previous condition of servitude. (February 3, 1870) There was something called the Enforcement Act of 1871 or also known as the Civil Rights act of 1871 where they basically shut the Ku Klux Klan and other organizations down no more combat hate crimes of any sort. Next you have the Civil Rights Act of 1875 or the Force Act. It was to guarantee African American equal treatment in public accommodations, public transportation, and prohibit exclusion from jury duty.

Few other Amendments I think you should be aware of:

First Amendment Prohibits Congress from making any law respecting an establishment of religion, impeding the free exercise of religion, impeding the freedom of the press, interfering with the right to peaceably assemble or prohibiting the petitioning for a governmental redress of grievances.(December 15, 1791)

Fifth Amendment Sets rules for indictment by grand jury and eminent domain, protects the right to due process, and prohibits self-incrimination and double jeopardy.(December 15, 1791)

My favorite because I am a woman and it was ratified on my birthday, The nineteenth Amendment prohibits the denial of the right to vote based on sex. (August 18, 1920)

You should know all 27 Amendments to the United States Constitution. I happened to just point out a few.

Bill of rights

Amended in 1689 is an Act of the Parliament of England that addresses constitutional matters and sets up certain basic civil rights to a person. Looking for a better understanding of where it stems from look up the Declaration of Rights.

Constitutional right

Is a right or freedom granted to U.S. citizens by our United States Constitution?

Knowledge about where you live

We live in North America our country is called The United States of America (U.S.A.), United States (U.S.), or America. The U.S. is the fourth biggest country in the world by land. We are made up of fifty states, five US territories, and one district. The U.S. territories being Guam, Puerto Rico, American Samoa, Virgin Island and Northern Mariana Island. While the one district being Washington D.C. the National Capital which isn't even a part of America. *How Sway How? That's just mind boggling* We don't have an official language isn't that crazy. We are one of the most religious countries in the western world. And African American music and culture is a big influence in America and around the world.

Get a passport go see the world!

The Pledge of Allegiance

"I pledge allegiance to the flag of the united states of America, and to the Republic for which it stands, one Nation under God, indivisible, with liberty and justice for all."

Pledge of Allegiance was created in 1887 by Colonel George Balch his expression of allegiance to the flag. It was adopted by Congress in 1942, it got its name in 1945 along with one last change adding the words "under God" When reciting the pledge stand at attention facing the flag with right hand over heart, if wearing a hat remove and hold over shoulder, and if uniformed solider salute.

Star Spangled Banner
The national anthem came from a poem called "Defense of Fort Henry" written by Francis Scott Key on September 14 1814. Was adopted the national anthem March 3 1931
"Oh, say, can you see, by the dawns early light,
What so proudly we hailed at the twilights last gleaming?
Whose broad stripes and bright stars, through the perilous flight,
For the ramparts we watched, were so gallantly streaming
And the rockets' red glare the bombs bursting in air
Gave proof through the night that our flag was still there
O says does that star spangled banner yet wave
For the land of the free and the home of the brave?"

America (my country tis of thee)
My country tis of thee sweet land of liberty of thee I sing land where my fathers died land of the pilgrims pride from every mountain side let freedom ring.

America, the Beautiful
Oh beautiful for spacious skies for amber waves of grain for purple mountains majesties above the fruited plain America god shed his grace on thee and crown thy good with brotherhood from sea to shining sea.

Declaration of Independence
was created around June or July of 1776 and ratified on July 4 1776 to announce and explain separation from Great Britain the United States of America was born. Nothing to do with our individual freedom, we are celebrating the United States being born as a country. It also contains some of the most potent words and best known sentence in American history. "We hold these

truths to be self-evident, that all men are created equal, that they are empowered by their Creator with certain unalienable Rights that among these are Life, Liberty and the pursuit of Happiness.

Federal Holidays
(The highlighted days I actually see a meaning worth celebrating)

1. **New Year's Day**: January 1st (wondering why anything new another chance is always worth celebrating)
2. **Martin Luther King Jr. Day**: 3rd Monday in January
3. Presidents Day: 3rd Monday in February
4. **Memorial Day**: Last Monday in May
5. Independence Day: July 4th
6. **Labor Day**: 1st Monday in September
7. Columbus Day: 2nd Monday in October
8. **Veterans Day**: November 11th
9. Thanksgiving: 4th Thursday in November
10. Christmas: December 25th

I'm not saying memorize and get ready to party all I'm saying is just know you might be owed time and a half on these days at work. LOL

The Statue of Liberty was made with Blacks in mind the original statue had broken chains at her feet and in her left hand, a tribute to Black Slaves and appreciation for being and playing a major role in winning the Civil War. You can see the original model of the statue of liberty at the Museum of the City of NY, Fifth Ave and 103rd Street.

Free emergency hotlines

Any immediate emergency needing assistance dial 911
Dial 211 or log onto www.211.org facilitated by united way
#77 from any phone connects you to the highway patrol
Dial 311 for any non-emergency question
Baby Safe Haven Hotline 18668147233
Independence House Hotline 18004396507
Domestic Violence Hotline 18007997233

Labor Law also known as the employment law or labor law is what set the expectations in a work environment and between workers and bosses alike. Everything from pay, hours, unions, child labor can be found under this law.

Schools that give free tuition Yes there are schools out there that will give you free tuition based off home/family income, being a veteran, or just committing to a service or something after graduation. New York recently in early 2017 started a Free-Tuition Program. Read up, search, and apply for scholarships/grants you never know who looking to finance someone with your attributes.

The United States Census Bureau is a the home of United States statistics a federal system that produces data about Americas people and the economy you can read up on census test and survey while checking the population based of race, sex, age or everyone as a whole. Check out census.gov the next big event is census 2020.

Bank accounts and stock and bonds Credit

maintaining building pale grants black investment groups Being American I'm sure everyone has pretty much seen what a dollar can do. Ultimately the goal is to capitalize off of something because just living to work will have you in the same spot forever. Being an American we need to know how to build a solid foundation for self and future descendants. A bank account for an expected child even if it's a dollar a day it adds up. Everyone needs a bank account or safe. Stocks and bonds are a great thing to watch grow them can be very profitable whether it be short or long term vesting. When dealing with credit I suggest whatever you have that may be attached to payments pay it on time or before, pay just a few dollars over, and try to keep it a quarter to half of the limit. Look into free money there are pale grants out there looking to give a specific description of a person or their goals free money. Look into it you never know it could be money out there with you name on it. Check out Angel Rich phone app the Credit Stacker a game by a sista that helps you to understand how credit works.

If you have debt, work on it making payments and paying just a little over your minimum before your due date helps your credit rise up. During tax season invest ten percent of your return into something profitable.

Discrimination: is the process by which two stimuli differing in some aspect are responded to differently. Highlighted difference of treatment between members of different groups when one is intentionally singled out and treated worse…racial gender sexual orientation. **2.** Treatment or consideration of, or making a distinction in favor of or against a person or thing based on the group, class, or category to which that person or thing belongs rather than on individual merit.

Did you know that police departments have quotas Blacks and Hispanics fourteen – twenty-one are targeted. It's illegal to have quotas

Social equality is a state of affairs in which all people within a specific society or isolated group have the same status in certain respects, including civil rights, freedom of speech, property rights and equal access to certain social goods and services

Racial Integration creating equal opportunity regardless of race and the development of a culture that draws on diverse traditions, rather than merely bringing a racial minority into the majority culture

Constitutional Right a liberty protected from government interference guaranteed by a constitution

Freedom the power or right to act, speak, or think as one wants without interference or restraint

Rights legal, social, or ethical principles of freedom or entitlement

Do you know your blood type if you needed blood do you know the type of blood you need to be saved or possibly even save someone? (I'm the universal donor so holla at me if you need me. Lol) No but on a serious note I am the Universal blood type O positive and did you know Native Americans and Aborigines were all one hundred percent O Positive before colonization just something to yet again think about.

The American dream

"That dream of a land in which life should be better and richer and fuller for everyone, with opportunity for each according to ability or achievement. It is a difficult dream for European upper classes to interpret adequately, and too many of us ourselves have grown weary and mistrusted of it. It is not a dream of motor cars and high wages merely, but a dream of social order in which each man and each woman shall be able to attain to the fullest stature of which they are innately capable, and be recognized by others for what they are, regardless of the fortuitous circumstances of birth or position."

"Life should be better and richer and fuller for everyone, with opportunity for each according to ability or achievement." **Unknown**
(Regardless of birth circumstances or social class)

American Dream: Noun; The ideal the every U.S. citizen should have an equal opportunity to achieve success and prosperity through hard work, determination, and initiative

Go look over
Constitutioncenter.org
Givemeliberty.org
Thelawdictionary.org

Can anyone explain to me "The Law That Never Was"

and let me know about if the IRS is really licensed in any state to do business and take our money? Asking for a friend. LOL

THEY CAN HELP YOU BETTER UNDERSTAND THE LAWS #YOUTUBE
Taj Tarik Bey
Queen Valahra Renita EL Harre Bey

OR GO WATCH
13TH (2016 Documentary)

OR GO READ
Black's Law Dictionary- Henry Campbell Black (1891)

> *"The Law is meant to be my servant, not my master, not my torturer and my murderer."*
>
> *James Baldwin*

Netta B.

NOTES

Netta B.

SOCIAL, CHARITY, EDUCATIONAL, SELF-HELP

This section is for you if you want to make a change with your life for your life or your children life. There is so much support and help out there as well as ways to help. Let's build TOGETHER.

Incite! Women of Color against Violence

Black Girls Rock, Inc. founded in 2006 with the mission "change the world by empowering Black girls to lead, innovate, and serve."

National Society of Black Engineers

Brown Girls Do, Inc. not-for-profit dedicated to promoting diversity in the arts by providing annual scholarships, a mentor network, and community programs to empower young girls.

National black chamber of Commerce

The Lopes Foundation

Girls Going Global Inc. nonprofit dedicated to empowering girls through travel and cultural exchange.

National black justice commission

Be Someone Inc. mission is to build character, hope, and inspiration so that kids can set and achieve lifetime goals, realize their full potential and be someone. Using the chessboard as a visual aid and the game is the key to success.

(WEEN) the Women in Entertainment Empowerment Network

Black Girls Code founded in 2011 "Imagine, build, create." Ultimate goal is to increase the number of women of color in the digital space by empowering girls of color 7-17 years of age to become innovators in STEM fields in their communities, and builders of theirs own futures through exposure to computer science and technology. To provide African American youth with the skills to occupy some of the 1.4 million computing job openings expecting to be available in the U.S. by 2020, and to train one million girls by 2040.

Blacks in Government

National Coalition of 100 Black Women advocates on behalf of black women and girls promoting leadership development and gender equity in health, education, and economic empowerment. Founded in New York in 1970

National Black MBA Association

United Negro College Fund founded in 1944 has helped over 445,000 students attend, thrive, graduate and become leaders.

National Medical Association

The Taylor Michaels Scholarship Program

Jack and Jill of America, Inc. founded in 1938 in Philadelphia, Pennsylvania for African American women made by middle and upper class women wanting to bring their children together for social, educational and cultural opportunities and experience which was not readily available to their children due to racism or segregation

DreamGrlz

The Steve and Marjorie Harvey Foundation

100 Black Men of America founded in New York City in 1963 made up of mostly black college degree black men who mission is to "Improve the quality of life within their communities and enhance educational and economic opportunities for all African Americans."

Keep a Child Alive

The DIVA Foundation

Sister Love, Inc. to eradicate the impact of HIV and sexual and reproductive oppressions upon all women and their communities in the U.S. and around the world

Common Ground Foundation

The LINKS, Incorporated this social service organization was founded in 1946 you have to volunteer X amount of hours.

Blackout for human rights

Color of Change founded 2005 is an online racial justice organization whose mission is to help people respond effectively to injustice in the world around us.

The Black Youth Project

Rush Philanthropic Arts Foundation

The Innocence Project founded in 1992 is committed to exonerating wrongly convicted people through the use of DNA testing OR in some cases where DNA testing was not possible and to reforming the criminal justice system to prevent future injustice.

#cut50

My Brother's Keeper (MBK) founded in 2015 with the vision to ensure all of the nation's young men of color have equal opportunity to achieve success and prosperity

We are here

The Girl Friends Incorporated founded during the Harlem Renaissance in 1927 **the Girls Griend Fund** founded in 1989

Netta B.

National black injustice coalition

National Urban League mission is to enable African Americans to secure economic self-reliance, parity, power, and civil rights.

The Empowerment Program

Purple Purse Program

The app- **NOTOK** created by the Lucas siblings to cope or help with suicidal thoughts

Are you familiar with THE
#MeToo Movement
#StandUpWithTamika

Nomore.org

Do You Know Your Status?
1800CDCINFO
HIV.GOV

LOOKING FOR DIFFERENT TOPICS OR POSSIBLY A ANSWER? MAYBE JUST FEELING OPEN MINDED HERE ARE SOME THINKERS.
#YOUTUBE

Speakers
Dr. Yosef Ben-Jochannan
Dr. Patricia Newton
Dr. Umar Abdullah Johnson
Dr. Frances Welsing
Sister Shahrazad Ali
Dr. Amos Wilson
Dr. Marimba Ani
Bobby Hemmitt
Dr. Claud Anderson
Mfundishi
Dane Calloway

Are you familiar with Derrick Grace?

Documentaries
The Secret of Selling the Negro Market (1954)
The New Negro (1957)
Black Liberation *Silent Revolution* (1967)
The Heritage of Slavery (1968)
The Black Woman (1970)
Accomplished Women (1974)
The New Girl in the Office 1960)

More of a movie person
Eyes on the Prize (1978)
The Pursuit of Happyness (2006)
Slavery by another Name (2012)
Hidden colors documentaries (2011)

For colored girls (2010)
The African Americans; Many Rivers To Cross (2013)
The World According to Monsanto (2008)
The Great Debaters (2007)
Raisin in the sun (1961)
12 Years a Slave (2013)
Ali (2001)
The Hurricane (1999)
The real eve documentary (2002)
Amistad (1997)
Selma (2014)
For Us, The Living (1983)
Marley (2012)
Higher Learning (1995)
Free Angela and all political prisoners (2012)
Get Out (2017)
Ghost of Mississippi (1996)
I am Not Your Negro (2016)
School daze (1988)
American Promise (2013)
Do the Right Thing (1989)
Ray (2004)
Marshall (2017)
Remember the Titans (2000)
The Help (2011)
Banished (2006)
The Black List (2008 documentary)
500 Years Later (2005)
Lean On Me (1989)
Hidden Figures (2016)
GMO-OMG (2013)
Life and Debt (2001)
The Black Power Mixtape (2011)
Black Panther (2018)

MELANIN

Wallstreet (1987)

For the reader in you
Arena Wendell Bontemps
Sterling Allen Brown
Countee Cullen
Ralph Waldo Ellison
Toni Morrison
Marcus Garvey
Daisy Bates
James Baldwin
Langston Hughes
Rudolph Fisher
Paul Dunbar
Wallace Thurman
Mya Angelou
Zora Neale Hurston
Sista Soulja
1oo Amazing Facts about the Negro with Complete Proof
Booker T. Washington "Up from Slavery" (1901)
William Cooper Nell "The Colored Patriots in American Revolution" with introduction by Harriet Beecher Stowe published in (1855)
"The state against Blacks" Walter E. Williams (1982)
David Barton "American History in Black and White" (2004)
The Four Agreements- Don Miguel Ruiz (1997)
Message to the Blackman in America- Elijah Muhammad (1965)
The Hate U Give- Angie Thomas (2017)
The Alchemist- Paulo Coelho (1988)
The New Jim Crow- Michelle Alexander (2010)

Dear Martin- Nic Stone (2017)
Negros with Guns- Robert F Williams (1962)
The American Negro- William Hannibal Thomas (1901)
The Original Black Elite: Daniel Murray and the Story of the Forgotten Era- Elizabeth Dowling Taylor (2017)
Black Bolshevik- Harry Haywood (1978)
The Destruction of Black Civilization- Chancellor (1971)
Post Traumatic Slave Syndrome- Joy DeGruy (2005)
A Taste of Power- Elaine Brown (1993)
Nigger- Dick Gregory (1964)
Isis Papers- Frances Cress Welsing (1982)
From Niggas to Gods- Akil (1993)
The Mis-Education of the Negro- Carter G. Woodson (1933)
Let me Live- Angelo Herndon (1937)
Revolutionary Suicide- Huey P. Newton (1973)
God, the Black Man and Truth- Ben Ammi Ben-Israel (1982)
Autobiography of Malcolm X (1965)
The Secret- Rhonda Byrne (2006)
The Odyssey of Black Men in America- Herb Boyd (1995)
Phillis Wheatley first African American to publish a book "Poems on Various Subjects, Religious and Moral (1773)
The Greater Exodus: An Important Penteheucal Criticism based on the Archaeology of Mexico and Peru- J Fitzgerald Lee (1903)

...The bible and Quran are good reads too sometimes you have to see beyond the painted picture.

<u>If you can find an old Encyclopedia or Dictionary from like the 1800's or early 1900's you would be</u>

surprised at what you see. I'm sure!

I love a Good Picture Book
Posing Beauty: African American Images from the 1890's to the Present
Unseen: Unpublished Black History from the New York Times Photo Archives
Dark Girls
National Museum of African American History and Culture: A Souvenir Book
Black: A Celebration of a Culture
Faces of Africa
Queens

Victor Hugo Green's The Green Book can be found online if you want to see some of the original Black friendly businesses

Search search search

Library of Congress- loc.gov
Digital Public Library of America- dp.la
National Archives- archives.gov
Smithsonianeducation.org

Support US

Eric Townsend is self-taught engineer who has made around two dozen apps one in particular I like to point out is BLVCK which has news that is catered to the Black community

supportblackeowned.com
blackbusiness.org
theblackpeoplematrix.com
blackenterprise.com
blackartdepot.com
webuyblack.com
nomeansnoworldwide.org

"None but ourselves can free our minds."

Bob Marley

MELANIN

Netta B.

NOTES

MELANIN

THE FUTURE IS BRIGHT

#Tony D. Hansberry
#Kimberly Anyadike
#Joshua Beckford
#Angel Rich
#Caleb Green (4yr reads 100 books a day)
#Zakiya Randall
#Kheris Rogers
#Zandra Cunnigham
#Anaya Lee Willabus
#Dorothy Jean
#Cori Gauff
#Marian Brown
#Kevin Stonewall
#Tre Taylor
#Rochelle Ballantyne
#Nancy Abu-Bonsrah
#Deddah Howard
#Essynce Moore

#Jahmir Smith
#Breanna Holbert
#Stephen Wiltshire
#Jasmine Stewart
#Cliffannie Forrester
#Charlie and Hannah Lucas
#Sandra Musujusu
#Silas Adekunle
#Tiffany Nicole Davis
#Simone Manuel
#Tera Poole
#Elaine Welteroth
#Ronnie Nelson Sidney
#Gabrielle Godwin
#Tyson Hobson-Powel
#Derek Onserio
#Esther Okade
#Ava Roberts
#Ramarni Wilfred
#Anala Beevers
#Jewel Jones
#Maame Biney

A Bright future needs a bright child
Find more reads under these authors

I Have a Dream- Kadir Nelson (Hardcover has Dr. Kings entire I Have a Dream speech official recording)
This is the Dream- Diane Z. Shore & Jessica Alexander
A is for Activist- Innosanto Nagara
Harlem's Little Blackbird- Renee Watson
Giant Steps to Change the World- Spike Lee &Tonya Lewis Lee

Netta B.

One Crazy Summer – Rita Williams-Garcia
Take a Picture of Me, James VanDerZee- Andrea Loney (Based on true events)
In Daddy's Arms I AM TALL
Each Kindness- Jacqueline Woodson
28 Days; Moments in History that Changed the World- William Smith (Based on True events)
The Boy Who Harnessed the Wind- Bryan Mealer & William KamKwamba (Based on true events)
Long Way Down- John Reynolds
Bippity Bop Barbershop – Natasha Tarpley
Full, full, full of love- Trish Cooke
American Street- Ibi Zoboi
Turning 15 on the Road to Freedom- Lynda Blackman Lowery (Based on true events)
The People Could Fly- Virginia Hamilton
Between the Lines- Sandra Neil Wallace
A Strong Right Arm- Michelle Y. Green (Based on true events)
A Dance Like Starlight- Kristy Dempsey (Based on true events)
Firebird- Misty Copeland (Based on true events)
Child of the Civil Rights Movement- Paula Young Shelton (based on true events)
Chocolate me- Taye Diggs & Shane W. Evans
The Blacker the Berry- Joyce Carol Thomas
Childtimes- Eloise Greenfield & Lessie Jones
Nelson Beats the Odds- Ronnie Sidney
Aya- Marguerite Abouet & Clement Oubrerie
Art from Her Heart- Clementine Hunter (Based on true events)
Ron's Big Mission- Rose Blue Corinne Naden (Based on true events)
Pass It On (African American Poetry for Children)

MELANIN

Peter's Chair- Ezra Jack Keats
Ruth and the Green Book- Calvin Alexander Ramsey & Gwen Strauss
The Story of Ruby Bridges- Robert Coles
Roll of Thunder, Hear My Cry- Mildred D. Taylor
We March- Shane W. Evans
The Other Side- Jacqueline Woodson
Baby says - John Steptoe
The Watsons Go to Birmingham- Christopher Paul Curtis
Sewing Stories- Barbara Herkert (Based on true events)
Wild, Wild Hair –Nikki Grimes
Tar Beach- Faith Ringgold
The Youngest Marcher- Cynthia Levinson (Based on true events)
Something Beautiful- Sharon Dennis Wyeth
Chains- Laurie Halse Anderson
Brown Girl Dreaming – Jacqueline Woodson
Before there was Mozart- Lesa Cline-Ransome (Based on true events)
Freedom on the Menu- Carole Boston Weatherford
The Barbers Cutting Edge- Gwendolyn Battle-Lavert
Freedom Summer- Deborah Wiles
Monster- Walter Dean Myers
Between the Lines- Sandra Neil Wallace (Based on true events)
A Sweet Smell of Roses- Angela Johnson
Glory Be- Augusta Scattergood (Based on true events)

*Afro-Bets Books by Wade Hudson and Valerie Wilson Wesley are awesome for teaching children Black

History*

A little home schooling never hurt anything

Tolerance.org
Commonsense.org

"We all grow, learn, and die but very few live... As long as you do what you want to be doing you living!"

Netta B.

MELANIN

QUOTES, SPEECHES, CONVERSATIONS

Now this is probably one of my favorite sections in the book. So you know how you can get a note or letter and its uplifting or eye opening and start feeling good all smiley then you fold the paper back up and stash it in a pocket or something until you cross paths with it again. That's why I love this section I hope you can find your one favorite or favorite quotes to keep or reflect on in a time of need. Yes I know they are just words but they are words with meaning depth truth above all encouragement. Maybe twice a day I'm seeking a uplifting encounter or challenge all while keeping me grounded. I know for a fact we are not all that different so here are yours.

Interviewer: Were you trying to provoke anybody to do anything in particular? Were you trying to...get people to do things?

Tupac: Yes!!
Interviewer: Tell us what.
Tupac: Think. Use ya head!

A Black Oath (A Pledge of Allegiance for Black People)

I pledge allegiance to my own black self-respect and to the respect of all other Black (and shades of Black) people on planet earth. All of whom are victims of the system of racism (white supremacy) and, I pledge to use all of my life, energy, intelligence and creativity, in all areas of people activity, to eliminate the global system of racism (white supremacy) on planet earth and to replace it with justice; so help me God.
Dr. Frances Cress Welsing ☐

"You can't lead the people if you don't love the people. You can't save the people if you don't serve the people." **Cornel West**

The Black Code

We DO NOT STEAL from one another.
We DO NOT KILL one another.
We DO NOT SELL or OFFER DRUGS to one another.
We DO COMBINE OUR DOLLARS and BUY COLLECTIVELY as a group.

We PROTECT OUR OWN, Women and Children FIRST.
We EDUCATE OUR OWN at every change.
We DO NOT FIGHT one another.
BROTHERS PROTECT and BUILD UP one another.
SISTERS PROTECT and BUILD UP one another.
We LOOK FOR EVERY OPPORTUNITY to START OUR OWN BUSINESS servicing the NEEDS OF OUR PEOPLE FIRST.

"We gotta stop teaching each other to accept the way things are and just *'go along with the get along'*. That's part of the reason why we are in this situation today. We have too many Black people that think it's beneficial for us to ignore our situation; not think about it, not talk about it, if we ever want to get somewhere, then we gotta make some damn noise. We can't get comfortable." **Assata Shakur**

Mother to Son
Well son, I'll tell you
Life for me ain't been no crystal stair
It had tacks in it,
And splinters,

And boards torn up
And places with no carpet on the floor bare,
But all this time
I'se been a climbin' on,
And reachin landin's
And turning corners,
And sometimes goin in the dark
Where there aint been no light,
So boy, don't you turn back.
Don't you set down on the steps
Cause you finds it kinder hard.
Don't you fall now, for I'se still going honey, I'se still climbin'
And life for me aint been no crystal stair.
Langston Hughes

"After the Emancipation Proclamation, when the system of slavery changed from chattel slavery to wage slavery, it was realized that the Afro-American constituted the largest homogeneous ethic group with a common origin and common group experience in the United States and, if allowed to exercise economic or political freedom, would in a short period of time own this country. Therefore racist in this government developed techniques that would keep the Afro-American people economically dependent upon the slave masters--economically slaves—

twentieth-century slaves." **Malcolm X**

"I don't know what the future may hold, but I know who holds the future." **Hosea Williams**

The African Pledge

We will remember the humanity, glory, and suffering of our ancestors and honor the struggle of our elders; We will strive to bring new value, and new life to our people. We will have peace and harmony among us, we will be loving, sharing, and creative. We will work, study, listen, so we may learn; learn so we may teach. We will cultivate self-reliance. We will struggle to resurrect and unify our homeland; we will raise children for our nation. We will have discipline, patience, devotion and courage. We will live as models; to provide new direction for our people. We will be free and self-determining. We are African people…We will win!!!

"We are oppressed because we are black. We must use that very concept to unite ourselves and to respond as a cohesive group. We must cling to each other with a tenacity that will shock the perpetrators of evil." **Steve Bantu Biko**

I Am The Black Child
I am special, Ridicule cannot sway me
I am strong, obstacles cannot stop me
I hold my head high, proudly proclaiming my uniqueness
I hold my pace, continuing forward through adversity
I am proud of my culture and my heritage
I am confident that I can achieve my every goal
I am becoming all that I can be
I am the Black child, I am a child of God.
Mychal Wynn

"Hate is a great burden to bear. It injures the hater more than it injures the hated." **Coretta Scott King**

Black Woman
Black woman with all your might,
Black woman you are truly a beautiful sight.
Black woman with your beautiful face,
You are definitely a credit to your black race.
Black, woman, say it loud
Being Black is being proud.
Black woman in this unbearable land,

Stop a minute and take your Black brothers hand
Black woman you are a mother, woman, and a friend
Without a Black woman a Black man cannot win
Black woman education and respect are your goal,
All these are said but seldom showed
Black woman, be proud of what you are
Because it will always take you very far
Black woman whose fore-parents were once a slave
If you apply you can have it made.
Black woman you are clean, modest, and neat,
Believe me Black woman you can't be beat.
Black woman always watch what you do
Being Black makes everyone else watch you
God made heaven, God made earth. Beautiful Black woman consider your-self… what God made first.
Wilton Antonio McGlory

"I have created nothing really beautiful, really lasting, but if I can inspire one of these youngsters to develop the talent I know they possess, then my monument will be in their work." **Augusta Savage**

Hey Black Child
Hey Black Child,
Do you know who you are?
Who you really are?
Do you know you can be,
What you want to be?
If you try to be,
What you can be.
Hey Black Child,
Do you know where you're going?
Where you're really going,
Do you know you can learn
What you want to learn?
If you try to learn,
What you can learn?
Hey Black Child,
Do you know you are strong?
I mean really strong?
Do you know you can do,
What you want to do?
If you try to do,
What you can do?
Hey Black Child,
Be what you can be.
Learn what you must learn.
Do what you can do.
And tomorrow your nation will be what you want it to be.
Useni Eugene Perkins

"Hold fast to dreams, for if dreams die, life is a broken-winged bird that cannot fly." **Langston Hughes**

Beautiful Black Man
Like a lion that stands over his pride
And his dominion over his land
You are fearfully and wonderfully made
Strong Beautiful Black Man.
You are centrifugal and driving force
That draws me deeply into you
You are everything that my heart desires
Your love I could never refuse
Even in those times when it seems
That the world knows not your name
I will always be there to remind you
Of your strength, your pride, and your fame
Though most personify fear of you
Because of what they do not know
For it is not what their eyes can see
But rather what their hearts truthfully know
That your abilities are limitless
Your hands can accomplish any task
Even when it seems impossible
You always manage to show contrast
I am only trying to reassure you

That I am the exception to the rule
That I will love you no matter what
Win, draw, or lose.
Even when you are feeling
That you have lost your place in this land
Sometimes being portrayed and even told
That you are less than a man
Don't you give into anger
Please don't hold your head down
Exhibit your strength and your pride
Remember, you wear a crown
Because you are still King amongst Kings
In my world, you are in high demand
Remember, I do love you no matter what
My Strong Beautiful Black Man!
Victoria Z

"If a man is not faithful to his own individuality, he cannot be loyal to anything." **Claude McKay**

We Real Cool
We real cool. We
Left school. We

Lurk late. We
Strike straight. We

Netta B.

Sing sin. We
Thin gin. We

Jazz June. We
Die soon.
Gwendolyn Brooks

"I don't condemn and I don't convert. I've been searching through books and bibles to find what this life is worth, and I've made up my mind: love is my religion. You can take it or leave it, and you don't have to believe it. Love is my religion."
Ziggy Marley

Incident
Once riding in old Baltimore,
Heart-filled, head-filled with glee,
I saw a Baltimorean
Keep looking straight at me.

Now I was eight and very small,
And he was no whit bigger,
And so I smiled, but he poked out
His tongue, and called me, "Nigger."

I saw the whole of Baltimore
From May until December;

Of all the things that happened there
That's all that I remember.
Countee Cullen

"I'm the daughter of a sister who's the mother of a brother who's the brother of another." **Queen Latifah**

"At a young age we are taught that Soul Food is the unhealthy death food that many of us put into our temples, but what is REAL Soul Food? Real Soul Food is food that enhances the Sol, our central sun, our melanin, our carbon. Fruits, vegetables, grains, this is the REAL Soul Food." **Dr. Sebi**

What is enough
Is persistence enough
Are words followed by action enough
Is consistency enough
Or are these things never enough
When did you have enough
And when should they say I've did what I can do
I did enough
Netta B.

"Be your true self because if you are not there are consequences to be paid." **Wendell Pierce**

"Failure: Is it limitation? Bad timing? It's a lot of things. It's something you can't be afraid of, because you'll stop growing. The next step beyond failure could be your biggest success in life." **Debbie Allen**

"I just tell the folks the truth. If they don't want truth, then don't come to moms." **Jackie "Moms" Mabley**

"There is a class of colored people who make a business of keeping the troubles, the wrongs, and the hardships of the Negro race before the public. Having learned that they are able to make a living out of their troubles, they have grown into the settled habit of advertising their wrongs- partly because they want sympathy and partly because it pays. Some of these people do not want the negro to lose his grievances, because they do not want to lose their jobs." **Booker T. Washington**

"Hungry people cannot be good at learning or producing anything, except perhaps violence." **Pearl bailey**

"We cannot discuss the state of our minorities until we first have some sense of what we are, who we are, what our goals are, and what we take life to be. The question is not what we can do now for the hypothetical Mexican, the hypothetical Negro. The question is what we really want out of life, for ourselves, what we think is real." **James Baldwin**

"There's always something to suggest that you'll never be who you wanted to be. Your choice is to take it or keep on moving." **Phylicia Rashad**

"I don't think it works to just be mad at them; Maxine Waters out ranting and kicking down the doors. It would be easy to dismiss you and marginalize you" **Maxine Waters**

"Failure is where all the lessons are." **Will Smith**

Choices
If I can't do what I want to do,
 Then my job is to
Not do what I don't want to do
It's not the same thing
But it's the best I can do.
If I can't have what I want
Then my job is to want what I've got
And be satisfied
That at least there is something more to want.
Since I can't go where I need to go
Then I must…
Go where the signs point
Through always understanding
Parallel movement isn't lateral.
When I can't express what I really feel
I practice feeling what I can express
And none of it is equal
I know
But that's why mankind alone
Among the animals learns to cry.
Nikki Giovanni

"Money and Success don't change people; they merely amplify what is already there." **Will Smith**

"When people saw what happened to my son, men stood up who had never stood up before." **Mamie Till-Mobley**

"You don't fight fire with fire. You fight fire with water. We're going to fight racism with solidarity were not going to fight capitalism with black capitalism were going to fight capitalism with socialism, socialism is the people if you're afraid of socialism you're afraid of yourself." **Fred Hampton**

"It is not the load that breaks you down, it's the way that you carry it." **Lena Horne**

"Fight me and you will bleed bad" **Sam McVea**

"Struggle is a never ending process freedom is never won you earn it and win it every generation." **Coretta Scott King**

"It's powerful, 'he said. "What?" That one drop Of Negro blood-because just one drop of black blood makes a man colored. One drop-you are a Negro!" **Langston Hughes**

"We need to focus on us as Black men and women and how we are virtually powerless without the other. We as Queens need to be the back bone for our Kings we need love trust respect and honesty embedded back into our relationships we need to rewind back to beauty being confidence strength and natural not naked and painted. Most importantly value ourselves as well as our men as we elevate the king in him by uplifting, supporting, calm and inspire him all with loyalty" **Netta B.**

"Black Women; You have been worshipped as a God for 1000's of years before the birth of Christ and much, much longer than you have been blamed for so called *original sin* and bringing pain and suffering into this world... you have a decision. Choose... A. Be a Goddess for yourself, family or somebody else and meet your real Divinity or... B. Be someone's blame, scapegoat, or worse." **Cody Norris**

"Sometimes I feel discriminated against but it

does not make me angry. It merely astonishes me. How can any deny themselves the pleasure of my company is beyond me" **Zora Neale Hurston**

"Fame will come just go be the greatest you through your efforts every single day and one day you'll get the opportunity because if you don't failure you won't know how to come back from failure can you come back from your lowest moment? And you didn't do the work you ain't coming back. So at the lowest levels work your hardest because one day you prepared for greatness, you're not preparing for a moment your preparing for greatness." **Marlon Wayans**

"It's time we stop worrying and get angry you know? But not angry and pick up a gun, but angry and open our minds." **Tupac**

"If you listen to people and if you allow people to project their fears on you, you won't live." **Taraji P Henson**

"I turned down one million though I had five

hundred left in the bank. I knew if Interscope were willing to pay one million. I could make forty million if I figured out how to own my talent." **Master P.**

What is Stability
Stability is a mind frame
Stability is havin all your bills paid
Stability is not wondering how your next meal will be made after you've just found a space where your head can be laid.
Stability is not worrying about your future
Because you're following the steps and plans for your particular goals
Your stability is not their stability
Their stability is not your stability
Stability is…
Netta B.

"I just try to get along with people and show the love that I would like to be shown to me." **Martin Lawrence**

"Whether you have a Ph.D., D.D. or no D, were in this bag together. And whether you are from Morehouse or Nohouse, we are still in this bag together." **Fannie Lou Hamer**

"Nothing is more important than stopping fascism because fascism will stop us all." **Fred Hampton**

"I'm black, I don't feel burdened by it and I don't think it's a huge responsibility. It's part of who I 'am. It does not define me." **Oprah Winfrey**

"I'm not concerned with your liking or disliking me…all I ask is that you respect me a human being" **Jackie Robinson**

"I had to make my own living and my own opportunity. But I made it! Don't sit down and wait for the opportunities to come. Get up and make them."
Madam C.J. Walker

"Eliminate the processed foods, the hybrid food, the GMO foods, eat only organic fruits and vegetables with seeds, which have a positive and not negative effect on your mucus membrane.

Anything without a seed is foreign created in a laboratory. Check before you eat. There's no harm in that. Stay strong people I'm with you." **Dr. Sebi**

"I knew then and I know when it comes to justice there is no easy way to get it." **Claudette Colvin**

"It's not who you are that holds you back, it's who you think you're not." **Jeal-Michel Basquit**

"It doesn't matter how strong your opinions are. If you don't use your power for positive change, you are, indeed, part of the problem." **Coretta Scott King**

"Ambition is priceless it's something that's in your veins and I doubt that ever change. Ambition is my shit and I put that on my name." **Wale**

"I'm in a season where I can't handle distractions I'm in a season were you either gotta be for me or against me and I don't really know what side you're going to choose but this on the bubble thing were we kind of friends but we not friends where you can talk about me and not treat me well and I just learn how to recover no I can't do that that's not for me no more I changed my mind see that's what dangerous about asking god to change your mind it starts kicking up dust in your life because all of sudden people preferred you when you were ignorant you preferred me when I was drunk and high and out of my mind you preferred me when I would just take anything and you could lie to me and cheat on me and say you would borrow money and never give it back you liked me better but when I started saying No when I started setting boundaries all of a sudden we got issues. Well God bless you I'm glad it's over. I not going to shrink myself to make you more comfortable" **Sarah Jakes Roberts**

"I wish I could say we were genius and say we were going to start our own company…that's not what happened in the beginning we went to every single label and every single label shut their door on us. The genius thing that we did was we didn't give up." **Jay Z**

"You do your best and you leave the rest. Don't let life drive you crazy you drive that motha fucka it's yours. You're in charge you can wait for something outside of you to help if you want you betta look in the mirror look in the mirror and love what you see or stand there until you love it if the tears come let them come but stand there…don't think is going to come over night. It's not! Your job is to do the work. Who I am?!"
Jennifer Lewis

I often feel like I have been a good person but I haven't done enough
I yearn for more so I self-sulk a lot.
Am I the only one who feels I don't have the outlet I wish I had,
do you have the support you wish you had?
You start to feel like the window of meeting the love of your life is closed. You feel like everything you passed up is haunting you.
You feel like every time you didn't listen to your gut OR instinct,
Now it all decides to crowd you.
You feel like the cool breezes and warm sun is now suffocating you.
You feel like the laughs and giggles are towards you.

I sometimes feel this way too.
I feel like what is, is not.
I went to a dark place but I see a light,
it's real little extremely tiny but I see it
I just have to climb
then I got to hop
and then I have to crawl and I think I'll be there.
I feel whatever that little speck of light is,
Represents all the laughs the giggles
the breeze the sun
all that is the real and not in my mind
that little light
that little speck
is where I can embrace what is and not what my thoughts make it to be.
That light is getting brighter and broader
I'm coming so close I need my shades.
Because its bright
I see a storm coming somehow I remembered to pack my umbrella
the storm is subsiding before I even get there
the sun is shining
I feel the warmth
I'm getting so close to the end and that cool breeze pushing those trees limbs I get a hint of air
I feel what's real
I don't feel my calves burning from the climb
I don't feel my nails hurting from almost falling

from that hop and digging my nails in the dirt
my knees and hands their not bleeding anymore
I feel a breeze
I see the light
I've crawled through that very dark tunnel
now I can stand
I stand tall and proud
I feel the love of the light breeze and smiles not laughs that were truly meant for me
I've made it and you can too.
  Netta B.

"You got to find out what you love then work harder than everyone else to be good at it, because it shouldn't feel like work if you really love it. Time you don't even feel time when you're doing something that you enjoy but when you're doing something you hate the shit moves crazy slow. I never seen nobody put in one hundred percent and lose…I see a lot of people that may be untalented but have the work ethic, they win. I see people that are very talented with no work ethic they lose and just be entitled and judgmental." **Damon Dash**

"Be not discouraged Black women of the world but push forward regardless of the lack of appreciation shown to you." **Amy Jacques Garvey**

"I frankly believe that every Negro in the country should learn judo and karate…If it's legal for a man to carry or have in his possession a rifle or shotgun especially faced with what Negros in this country are confronted with they should have it. They shouldn't go out attacking someone with it but in the face of brutality that face our people encounter it's not unjust to teach a negro to have a shotgun or rifle in their house…" **Malcolm X**

"I think you know…you know what you're supposed to do, deep down inside I think everybody does a lot of people just don't go after it you know. Most people start out I want to be a this but I'm going to be a that to fall back on and what your doing is your setting yourself up for failure cause you're going there's a possibility that I'm a fall back and when you put that out there then you fall back but if just say this what I want this is what I'm gonna do you usually get your stuff the way you want it." **Eddie Murphy**

☐

"Let us gear ourselves to the great task of

mapping out a pathway that will truly lead to a better world for us all." **Mary McLeod Bethune**

"At what point are we going to stop imitating imitators? You are imitating someone who is imitating you." **John Henrik Clarke**

"In order for us as poor and oppressed people to become part of a society that is meaningful, the system under which we now exist has to be radically changed… it means facing a system that does not lend it-self to your needs and devising means by which you change the system." **Ella Baker**

"The Negro wants to be everything but himself… He wants to integrate with the white man, be he cannot integrate with himself or with his own kind. The negro wants to lose his identity because he does not know his own identity." **Elijah Muhammad**

"Early in the day to know who you are you have to know who you are not and when you find out who you are you'll find out who everybody…

you have to understand that God start from within, I say get God." **Ceelo Green**

"I feel safe in the midst of my enemies, for the truth is all powerful and will prevail." **Sojourner Truth**

"There is a heaven, forever, day by day, the upward longing of my soul doth tell me so. There is a hell, I'm quite sure: for pray, if there were not, where would my neighbors go?" **Paul Laurence Dunbar**

"They want us to have amnesia to forgive and forget when it comes to any Black or African American related event or person. People spend all kinds of money to keep us quiet and lost in our own trance when it comes to media and us being consumers also" **Netta B.**

"Life is really short, so you add up all your traveling add up all your sleeping add up all your school add up all your entertainment you probably been half your life doing noting" **Muhammad Ali**

"I'm always thinking about creating my future starts when I wake up in the morning… Every day I find something creative to do with my life." **Miles Davis**

"Blessed to see another day to live out my purpose in life." **Keven Stonewall**

"We need the Black men in our homes because they provide guidance, protection, direction, instruction, discipline, gratification, and fulfillment, which a lot of Black women are pretending they don't even need no more." **Shahrazad Ali**

"Two months ago I had a nice apartment in Chicago. I had a good job. I had a son. When something happened to the Negros in the south I said, 'That's their business, not mine.' Now I know how wrong I was. The murder of my son has shown me that what happens to any of us, anywhere in the world, had better be the business of us all." **Mamie Till-Mobley**

"I had some great things and I had some bad things. The best and the worst…in other words, I had a life." **Richard Pryor**

"And then I got to Memphis. And some began to say the treats… or talk about the treats that were out. What would happen to me from some of our sick white brothers? Well I don't know what will happen now. We've got some difficult days ahead. But it doesn't matter with me now. Because I've been to the mountain top. And I don't mind. Like anybody, I would like to live a long life. Longevity has its place. But I'm not concerned about that now. I just want to do Gods will. And he will allow me to go up top the mountain. And I've looked over. And I've seen the promise land. I may not get there with you. But I want you to know tonight, that we, as a people, will get to the promise land! And so I'm happy, tonight. I'm not worried about anything. I'm not fearing any man. My eyes have seen the glory of the coming of the lord!" **Martin Luther King Jr.** (last speech on the day before his assassination)

"No people in the world profess so high a

respect for liberty and equality as the people of the United States, and yet no people hold so many slaves, or make such great distinctions between man and man." **Rev. Peter Williams Jr. (this is our country)**

"If we were made in his image then call us by our names most intellects do not believe in God but they fear us just the same." **Erykah Badu**

"Every natural resource that's keeping every country operating its sources is pulling from Africa. Everyone is benefiting but Africa. Africa doesn't need to be saved Africa is the one doing the saving." **Akon**

"The conqueror writes history; they came, they conquered, they write. You don't expect people who came to invade us to write the truth about us. They will always write negative things about us and they have to do that because they have to justify their invasions in all our countries." **Miriam Makeba**

"Water from the white fountain didn't taste any

better than from the black fountain." **B.B. King**

"We can say "peace on earth". We can sing about it or pray about it, but if we have not internalized the mythology to make it happen inside us, then it will not be." **Betty Shabazz**

"Look to Africa, when a black man shall be crowned, for the day of deliverance is at hand." **Marcus Garvey**

"I never really look for anything what God throws my way comes. I wake up in the morning and which every way God turns my feet I go." **Pearl Bailey**

"If all you can do is judge a person by their appearance because you don't have the spirit to judge someone from within you're in trouble." **Dick Gregory**

"Strive to be a woman of substance! Don't solely allow your big butt, thick thighs, wide hips, large breast, and overall good looks to define you as a woman. Your looks alone shouldn't define who you are. What more do you have to offer? What is your true Character? How is your attitude? What have you accomplished? Do you have respect for yourself? What do you represent? Everywhere you look, there's another beautiful, stunning, fine looking sista. Stand out from the rest dare to be different! Your good looks should only be a bonus, not the main factor." **Stephanie Lahart**

"The media's the most powerful entity on Earth. They have the power to make the innocent guilty and to make the guilty innocent, and that's power because they control the minds of the masses." **Malcolm X**

"If Black people were aware of their glorious past, then they would be more inclined to respect themselves." **Marcus Garvey**

"If you want to excel in something you learn it by studying it never giving up. So if you want to win in life, know life. Keep an open-mind while learning the set ups and ways to jump the hurdle expect the expected" **Netta B**

"There's no excuse for the young people not knowing who the heroes and heroines are or were." **Nina Simone**

"Money can't buy life" **Bob Marley**

"A Jewish business man told me; We call you Black People liquid money. The same way that water falls out of a man hands, money typically seeps out of a black persons hands the same way. Your community gets money and immediately gives it all away to people who aren't Black. We see that as a huge business opportunity." **Damon Dash**

9 Times Out of 10
Nine times out of ten
The harm done to someone is from family friends or acquaintance
Nine times out of ten
It's for personal reasons
Nine times out of ten
They wanted or needed you to need them alongside of them needing you

Nine times out of ten
You already knew this
Nine times out of ten.
Netta B.

"Was I always going to be here? No. I was not. I was going to be homeless at one time, a taxi driver, truck driver, or any kind of job that would get me a crust of bread. You never know what's going to happen." **Morgan Freeman**

"Virtue knows no color line…" **Ida B. Wells**

"I don't think it matters what I believe, only what I do." **Jackie Robinson**

"Look closely at the present you are constructing, it should look like the future you are dreaming." **Alice Walker**

"Historically, slavery was the worst thing to ever happen to a people and most slavery was mental, rather than physical. One of the biggest side effects of slavery is the fact that it made us afraid to take responsibility for our own destiny. Many brother and sisters today still do not want the responsibility that comes with nationalism and true revelation." **Dr. Umar Johnson**

"Whatever we believe about ourselves and our ability comes true for us." **Susan L. Taylor**

"God intends for you to live a life with no Ceilings. That ceiling in your life is not real. It has been manufactured by your fears." **Deric Muhammad**

Some of you can't even see me
Don't understand me
And never even felt me
I put your feelings and wants before mines
I follow your lead and change my direction
I'll let you go
Hopefully you'll come back to me
I'll never stop praying for you
And you'll never be forgotten
But since you can't see me
Will you remember me? ...Love
Netta B.

"Our nation is a rainbow- red, yellow, brown, black, and white- and we are all precious in Gods sight." **Jesse Jackson**

"My mother taught me that when you stand in truth and someone tells a lie about you, don't fight it." **Whitney Houston**

"Knowledge is not enough to change the conditions of Black people. Understand that we need to create programs and systems that will empower us economically, spiritually, and mentally. We need courage and action." **Nganga Njuranga**

"Greatness is not measured by what a man or woman accomplishes, but by the opposition he or she has overcome to reach his goals." **Dorothy Height**

"These kids out here listening to us and looking up to us cause a lot of them don't have no father figure in they house. And record you get on you lying talking bout some squares, get off of it man cause if you gone talk about some squares and talk about the drug game you need to talk about the bad side of the drug game too what about when you get dusted and you go to jail what about when you momma and yo wife and yo kids is crying cause they at home and you in prison in cell. Everybody talking about how many cars and how many jewels they gone buy....but ain't nobody talking bout the other side of it so if you gone talk about that you gotta talk about both sides cause the way we started is the way we gone finish." **Pimp C**

"You don't have to like everybody but you have to love everybody." **Fannie Lou Hamer**

"I am of the African race and in the colour which is natural to them of the deepest dye; and it is under a sense of the most profound gratitude to the supreme ruler of the Universe." **Benjamin Banneker**

"Don't let anyone rob you of your imagination, your creativity, or your curiosity. It's your place in the world: it's your life. Go on and do all you can with it, and make it the life you want to live."

Mae Jemison

"I can accept failure. Everyone fails at something. But I can't accept not trying." **Michael Jordan**

"A woman is free if she lives by her own standards and creates her own destiny, if she prizes her individuality and puts no boundaries on her hopes for tomorrow." **Mary McLeod Bethune**

"You can kill a man, but you can't kill an idea" **Medgar Evers**

"Bigotry and judgment are the height of insecurity." **Jasmine Guy**

"I was just trying to give my people a myth to live by." **Alex Haley**

"Loving one's self isn't hard, when you understand who and what yourself is. It has nothing to do with the shape of your face, the size of your eyes, the length of your hair or the quality of your clothes. It's so beyond all of those things and it's what gives life to everything about you. Your own self is such a treasure." **Phylicia Rashad**

"Don't chase your dream manifest it you know you chasing your dream you're never going to catch it you know just manifest it out your trust in a higher source and it'll manifest in your life." **Eddie Griffin**

"Only until all human beings begin to recognize themselves as human beings will prejudice be gone forever. People ask me what race I am, but there is no such thing as race. I just answer: "I'm a member of the human race." **Amelia Platts Boynton**

"To control a people you must first control what they think about themselves and how they regard their culture. When your oppressors make you ashamed of yourselves and culture, they no longer need chains to hold you." **Dr. John Henrik Clarke**

"The lady with the lamp, the Statue of Liberty, stands in New York Harbour. Her back is squarely turned on the USA. It's no wonder, considering what she would have to look upon. She would weep if she had to face this way." **Claudia Jones**

"I Am America. I am the part you won't recognize. But get used to me. Black confident cocky; my name not yours; my religion, not yours; my goals, my own; get used to me." **Muhammad Ali**

"Bringing in the gifts that my ancestors gave, I 'am the dream and hope of the slave. I rise I rise I rise" **Maya Angelou**

"I don't know the key to success, but the key to failure is trying to please everybody." **Bill Cosby**

"Some people don't want to marry within or have anything to do with their race because sometimes it stems from deep down in the blood line or it's a horrible experience that just sits and weighs on them able to just manifest so deeply that when quote unquote brother or sister says or does something to push and turn that dagger just a little deeper. We call each other names of what our race before us slave masters and owners called them. We quickly point out and make fun of features that slaves masters made fun of on a particular slave, the very same features someone in your family maybe 80 percent of your family members may have. These features are something that separates us from every other race while being clear signs or our past and true ancestor's story. I feel like we are consistently competing with each other because a slave owner decided to separate skin tones, because a slave master was able to make a strong black young able man look weak and defeated in front of his mother child wife or whomever and now those love ones who witnessed it harbor hate for the white man particularly but is more a product of being frightened while hate and resentment goes to the black man for not killing or stopping him but how can a man chained down stop anything? We are literally still chained down." **Netta B.**

"Life isn't a race, it's a relay." **Dick Gregory**

"...all girls rock but black girls we are on a whole notha level!" **Rihanna**

""Dipped in chocolate, bronzed in elegance, enameled with grace, toasted with beauty. My Lord, she's a black woman." **Dr. Yosef Ben-Jochannan**

"You're not a African because you're born in Africa. You're an African because Africa is born in you. It's in your genes… your DNA… your entire biological makeup. Whether you like it or not, that's the way it is. However if you were to embrace this truth with open arm, my, my, my, what a wonderful thing." **Marimba Ani**

"we are mentally a slave we are slave to brands we in slave to like a been symbol, we enslaved to chains a woman is enslaved to the concept that diamonds are a girl's best friend like girls in London don't even wear engagement rings that's all been programmed into us. When we born we born artist we born free and then we held down by society's perception of us we just don't want to be embarrassed." **Kanye West**

"Healing begins where the wound was made." **Alice Walker**

"I don't make records for pleasure. I did when I was a younger artist, but I don't today. I record so that I can feed people what they need, what they feel. Hopefully, I record so that I can help someone overcome a bad time." **Marvin Gaye**

"When you take care of yourself, you're a better person for others. When you feel good about yourself, you treat others better." **Solange Knowles**

"The Universal Zulu Nation stands to acknowledge wisdom, understanding, freedom, justice, and equality, peace, unity, love, and having fun, work, overcoming the negative through the positive, science, mathematics, faith, facts, and the wonders of God, whether we call him Allah, Jehovah, Yahweh, or Jah." **Afrika Bambaataa**

"The little life message I get from Cinderella, be

kind, be nice, good things will come to you and I started to realize that that's really what life is really made of its not made off the money it's not made of the cars it's not made of the jewels it's made off of the way you can make people feel and the ways people can make you feel it's about the love we can share the things we can create and when we do those things that's when we then become limitless." **Keke Palmer**

"You want to be successful keep two things in mind, hustle and patience. Do you any of the two?" **Netta B**

"The government brainwash our people with the mind control theory. That's what they do. They keep playing that same song, same song keep playing you start to like it…you start to get cloned wit it so therefore the clone exist and it takes over, it takes over the human body it takes over the spirit it takes over the soul and there for behold that's what you got." **Ol Dirty Bastard**

"People get used to anything. The less you think about your oppression, the more your tolerance for it grows. After a while, people just think oppression is the normal state of things. But to become free, you have to be acutely aware of being a slave." **Assata Shakur**

"I just played the sport because I loved it and because of the work I put into it next thing you know success was kind of bestowed upon me without me actually chasing it. It just happened." **Michael Jordan**

"Everybody wants to do something to help, but nobody wants to be first." **Pearl Bailey**

"Powerful people cannot afford to educate the people they oppress…because once you are truly educated, you will not ask for power. You will take it." **John Henrik Clarke**

"Challenges make you discover things about yourself that you never really knew." **Cicely Tyson**

"The future belongs to those who prepare for it today." **MalcolmX**

"We have a powerful potential in our youth, and we must have the courage to change old ideas and practices so that we may direct their power towards good ends." **Mary McLeod Bethune**

"What is the secret of eternal youth?
The answer is easily told:
All you gotta do if you wanna look young
is hang out with people who are old
if you ever go out with a school teacher,
you're in for a sensational night:
shell make you do it over and over again
until you do it right
the young people are very different today:
and there's one sure way to know:
kids used to ask where they come from:
now they'll tell you where to go!" **Nipsey Russell**

"It is our duty to fight for our freedom it is our duty to win we must love each other and support each other we have nothing to lose but our chains." **Assata Shakur**

"I refuse to follow those rules that society has set up. And the way that they control people with low self-esteem with improper information, with branding with marketing. I refuse to follow those rules it's about truth it's about information it's about awesomeness and the only luxury is time." **Kanye West**

"When I was in School, my mother stressed education. I am so glad she did. I graduated from Yale College and Yale University with my masters and I didn't do it by missing school." **Angela Bassett**

"Never underestimate the power of dreams and the influence of the human spirit. The potential for greatness lives within each of us." **Frederick Douglass**

"The most common way people give up their power is by thinking they don't have any." **Alice Walker**

"One thing we know about oppressed people when you can't enjoy true freedom you surround

yourself by the symbols of that freedom… that's why the Louie bag is so important that's why our kids will kill for Air Jordan's it's not the sneaker it's the status and if I believe I'm worthless that means I can only add value to myself by what I put on my body as opposed to what I put in it."
Dr. Umar Johnson

Competition
In the mirror all smiles to my competition
Winking at her
Cause she know I'm on a fucking mission
She told me don't worry bout these bitches reaching for your attention
They just bothered you don't see em as competition
Or reaching for their simple minded attention
Stay too yourself and do ya thang
Them hoe and Bitch made Negus gone be mad anyway.
Netta B.

"Stereotypes do exist, but we have to walk through them" **Forest Whitaker**

"Generally speaking I think we live in a world

that enjoys black culture and dislikes black people." **Cecil Emeke**

"I consider myself a crayon. I might not be your favorite color, but one day you're going to need me to complete your picture." **Lauryn Hill**

"Believe in yourself and don't let no one stop you from doin what you gotta do you gotta have faith if you can't find faith in the world find faith in God find faith in yourself but you gotta have faith." **Tupac**

"I have always thought that what is needed is the development of people who are interested not in being leaders as much as in developing leadership in others." **Ella Baker**

"Black folks, teach your children that they are direct descendants of the greatest and proudest race who ever peopled the earth. And it is because of the fear of our return to power, in a civilization of our own, that may outshine others, why we are hated and kept down by a jealous and prejudiced contemporary world." **Marcus**

Garvey

"You don't make progress by standing on the sidelines, whimpering and complaining. You make progress by implementing ideas." **Shirley Chisholm**

"No one is perfect in this imperfect world" **Patrice Lumumba**

"Be honest, brutally honest. That is what is going to maintain relationships." **Lauryn Hill**

"Build businesses do for self" **Marcus Garvey**
"No man can ever be what god intended him or her to be if you allow anything but God to make you afraid…anytime we allow anything to make us afraid and we refuse to challenge our fear of that thing then we can never be that man or that woman that god intended us to be because fear will not allow you to be yourself." **Louis Farrahkan**

"I finally face the fact that it isn't a crime not

having friends. Being alone means you have fewer problems." **Whitney Houston**

"Read through at least one book every week separate and distinct from your newspapers and journals it will mean that at the end of the year you will have read fifty-two different subjects. After five years you will have read over two hundred and fifty books. You may consider that a well-read man or well-read woman and there will be a great difference between you and the person who has not read one book. You will be considered intelligent and the other person be considered ignorant. You and that person therefore will be living in two different worlds; one the world of ignorance and the other the world of intelligence. Never forget that intelligence rules the world and ignorance carries the burden." **Marcus Garvey**

"We cannot afford to be separate…We have to see that all of us are in the same boat." **Dorothy Height**

"I can't build myself by beating somebody down" **Bernie mac**

"If our people are to fight their way up out of bondage we must arm them with the sword and the shield and buckler of pride-belief in themselves and their possibilities, based upon a sure knowledge of the achievements of the past." **Mary McLeod Bethune**

"We are not a problem people, we are people with problems." **Dorothy Height**

"No one is born hating another person because of the color of his skin or his background or his religion. People must learn to hate and if they can learn to hate they can be taught to love for love comes more naturally to the human heart than its opposite." **Nelson Mandela**

What is lonely?
I'll tell you what my lonely is
lonely is a longing
lonely is a need
lonely can only be fulfilled within self
the things that you want
the things you use

the things you crave
that's the filler it's not true to feed your lonely.
Only you know your lonely
your need your empty spot
when someone says their lonely they can mean so many things
from a desire to fulfill a goal
from a desire to sell a story
to just complete something can be their lonely
in order to fill your lonely
you need to know and understand your lonely
it's not that thing that you think you need right now
it's that thing you're trying to complete or obtain
once you gain knowledge of self and patience and control worldly discipline for self then you can begin to fill your lonely.
Netta B

"I find, in being black, a thing of beauty: a joy: a strength: a secret cup of gladness." **Ossie Davis**

"Keep working hard and you can get anything that you want." **Aaliyah**

"If you're going through a tough time, have faith

things will get better and always be willing to outwork your competition because you never know were life is gonna take you." **Dwayne Johnson** *"The Rock"*

"In order to see where we are going, we not only must remember where we have been, but we must understand where we have been." **Ella Baker**

"Change will not come if we wait for some other person or some other time. We are the ones we've been waiting for. We are the change that we seek." **Barack Obama**

"Were the only people on this entire planet who have been taught to sing and praise our demeaning. I'm a Bitch. I'm a Hoe. Ima a Gangster. I'm a Thug. I'm a Dog. **IF YOU CAN TRAIN PEOPLE TO DEMEAN AND DEGRADE THEMSELVES, YOU CAN OPPRESS THEM FOREVER**. You can even program them to kill themselves, and they won't even understand what happened." **Dr. Frances Cress Welsing**

"I know it seems hard sometimes but remember one thing through every dark night there's a bright day after that so no matter how Hard it get stick your chest out keep your head up and handle it." **Tupac Shakur**

"You must never be fearful about what you are doing when it is right," **Rosa Parks**

"Only a fool would support a culture that encourages him to disrespect his woman, buy things that he can't afford. Sell each other drugs and fill up the prisons. Calls you nigga, and your daughter a hoe. The white man doesn't have to lift a finger to oppress you because you're doing his job for him." **Malcolm X**

"Remember, we are not fighting for the freedom of the negro alone, but for the freedom of the human spirit a larger freedom that encompasses all mankind." **Ella Baker**

"…the press is manipulating everything that's been happening…they don't tell the truth. They are lying. They manipulate our story books. The history books are not true. It's a lie. The history books are lying you need to know that, you must know that." **Michael Jackson**

"You may write me down in history
With your bitter twisted lies
You may trod me in the very dirt
But still like dust I rise
Does my sassiness upset you
Why are you beset with gloom
Cause I walk like I got oil wells
Pumping in my living room
Just like moons and just like suns
With the certainty of tided
Just like hopes springing high
Still I rise
Did you want to see me broken
Bowed head and lowered eyes
Shoulders falling down like teardrops
Weakened by my soulful cries
Does my haughtiness offend you
Don't you take it awful hard
Cause I laugh like I got gold mines
Digging in my own backyard
You may shoot me with your words
You may cut me with your eyes
You may kill me with your hatefulness

But still like air I rise.
Does my sexiness upset you
Does it come as a surprise
That I dance like I got diamonds
At the meeting of my thighs
Out of the huts of history shame
I rise
Up from the past that's rooted in pain
I rise
I'm a black ocean leaping and wide
Welling and swelling I bear in the tide
Leaving behind nights of terror and fear
I rise
Into a daybreak that wondrously clear
I rise
Bringing the gifts that my ancestors gave
I am the dream and the hope of the slave
I rise
I rise
I rise."
Maya Angelou

"If you can't figure out your purpose, figure out your passion. For your passion will lead you right into your purpose." **T.D. Jakes**

"The greatest gift is not being afraid to question"

Ruby Dee

"Majority doesn't rule. One person can change the history of the world." **Paul Mooney**

"Our history is a passion for me. I feel that we leave out so much information and huge gaps in the American story and it makes it hard for people to really understand that we are all intricately related as Americans." **Jasmine Guy**

"Don't remove the kinks from your hair. Remove them from your brain." **Marcus Garvey**

"We must become members of a new race, overcoming petty prejudice, owing our ultimate allegiance not to nations but to our fellow men within the human community." **Ossie Davis**

"Our feelings are our most genuine paths to knowledge."
Audre Lorde

"I guarantee that the seed you plant in love, not matter how small will grow into a mighty tree of refuge. We all want a future for ourselves and we must now care enough to create nurture and secure a future for our children." **Afeni Shakur**

"Is it a crime, to fight, for what is mine?" **Tupac Shakur**

"Don't wait around for other people to be happy for you. Any happiness you get you've got to make yourself." **Alice Walker**

"You know, you don't see with your eyes. You see with your brain, and the more words your brain has. The more you can see." **KRS-ONE**

"Struggle is strengthening. Battling with evil gives us the power to battle evil even more." **Ossie Davis**

"everyone has the impulse to be elite." **Alfre Woodard**

"The American dream is built on a black nightmare. Every immigrant group finds a way to nestle into the black community to take from us whatever they need to build their communities, and exalt themselves in the fabric of America."
Louis Farrakhan

"Not failure, but low aim is a crime." **Roger Arliner Young**

Allowables
I killed a spider
Not a murderous brown recluse
Nor even a black widow
And if the truth were told this
Was only a small
Sort of papery spider
Who should have run
When I picked up my book
But she didn't
And she scared me
And I smashed her

I don't think
I'm allowed

To kill something

Because I am
Frightened
Nikki Giovanni

"Ignorance allied with power is the most ferocious enemy Justice can have." **James Baldwin**

"Once you know who you are you don't have to worry anymore." **Nikki Giovanni**

"If you dare to struggle you dare to win if you dare not to struggle then damn it you don't deserve to win." **Fred Hampton**

"Yesterday is gone. Tomorrow may be for us it may not." **Della Reese**

"Neither the republican nor democratic party can do for the colored race what they can do for themselves. Respect Black!" **Henry McNeal Turner**

"I thank God for correction and for hardships because it shows me where I am, where I was and where I need to be." **Lauryn Hill**

"Everybody shines, in different things. A lot of things I can't do, I can't play basketball...but I can act I know how to go to that true spot in myself cause I'm there every day. I can be me I can be whoever cause I'm true to me, I can go to neutral easily. A lot of people Black White Mexican young or old fat or skinny have a problem being true to they self, they have a problem looking in the mirror and looking directly in their own soul. The reason I sell six million records the reason I can go to jail and come out without a scratch the reason I can walk the reason I am who I am today is because I can look directly into my face and see my soul." **Tupac**

"No more self-limiting beliefs own your brilliance." **Jourdan Dunn**

"you keep watching them before you know it

time and life will be lost and you will have missed every opportunity that presented itself. Don't overlook your own blessing trying to figure someone else out." **Netta B.**

"If we must die, let it not be like hogs hunted and penned in an inglorious spot, while round us bark the mad and hungry dogs, making their mock at our accursed lot. If we must die, O let us nobly die, so that our precious blood may not be shed in vain that even the monsters we defy shall be constrained to honor us through dead. O Kinsmen. We must meet the common foe. Through far outnumbered let us show us brave and for their thousand blows deal one deathblow. What though before us lies the open grave? Like men well face the murderous, cowardly pack, pressed to the wall, dying, but fighting back!" **Claude McKay**

"We are not satisfied and we will not be satisfied until justice rolls down like waters and righteousness like a mighty stream." **Dr. MLK**

"Won't it be wonderful when black history and Native American History and all of U.S. History is taught from one book. Just U.S. history" **Maya Angelou**

"I have learned over the years that when one's mind is made up, this diminishes fear, knowing what must be done does away with fear." **Rosa Parks**

"I just played a sport because I loved it and because of the work that I put into it next thing you know success was kind of bestowed upon me without me actually chasing it, it just happened." **Michael Jordan.**

"There's always someone asking you to underline one piece of yourself- whether it's Black, woman, mother, dyke, teacher, etc., - because that's the piece that they need to key into. They want to dismiss everything else." **Audre Lorde**

"Black men struggle with masculinity so much. The ideas that we must always be strong really presses us all down- it keeps us from growing." **Donald Glover**

"By any means necessary" **Malcolm X**

"Everybody is a product of their environment. So before I could get mad at my daddy I had to stop and think what the hell did his momma do to him? And what the hell did her momma do to her? And so on and so forth. Somebody's got to be smart enough to break the cycle because I don't need my kids talking about me like that someday." **Lisa "Left Eye" Lopez**

"Motown was about music for all people – white and black, blue and green, cops and robbers. I was reluctant to have our music alienate anyone." **Berry Gordy**

"He who steals your past will control your future." **Unknown**

"I guess if I'd had any sense, I'd have been a little scared- but what was the point of being scared? The only thing they could do was kill me, and it kinda seemed like they'd been trying to do that a little bit at a time since I could remember."

Fannie Lou Hamer

"A minimum of comfort is necessary for the practice of virtue." **Patrice Lumumba**

"We as Black people have to tell our own stories. We have to document our history. When we allow someone else to document our history the history becomes twisted and we get written out. We get our noses blown off." **Erykah Badu**

"Sometimes I start to think that the hip audience ain't that intelligent sometimes you know where they don't pick up on it because they let the corniest shit get the most airplay the most unconscious shit get the most airplay." **Method Man**

"I am a woman who came from the cotton fields of the South. From there I was promoted to the washtub. From there I was promoted to the cook kitchen. And from there I promoted myself into the business of manufacturing hair goods and preparations…I have built my own factory on my own ground." **Madam C.J. Walker**

"When I grind I think about the family the fruits of labor to soon come. When you grind you think about your enemies and haters. You can't build like that because those people aren't gone ever let you have or give you your props. So that's how you're influenced and working for "The Man" Who is "The Man"? Your assumed competition and/or enemy and the puppeteer that puts all these images of success and realness in front of you." **Netta B.**

"I have found people on both sides of the aisle, white and black, that'll give you the shirt off their back, And I've also found people that won't give you a piece of bread if you're starving to death." **Al Green**

"Success doesn't come to you...you go to it." **Marva Collins**

"It is a call for black people in this country to unite, to recognize their heritage, to build a sense of community. It is a call for black people to define their own goals, to lead their own organizations." **Stokely Carmichael**

"There was no person, whether they thought I was too fat, too black, too country, too ghetto, too New York, too thug or too whatever. Nobody ultimately had to say over whether or not I was going to make it." **Kelly Price**

"Without dignity there is no liberty, without justice there is no dignity, and without independence there are no free men." **Patrice Lumumba**

"Sometimes you've got to let everything go – purge yourself…if you are unhappy with anything, whatever is bringing you down, get rid of it. Because you'll find that when you're free, your true creativity, you're true self comes out." **Tina Turner**

"Boycott your oppressor" **Martin Luther King Jr**

"Keep working hard and you can get anything

you want. If God gave you a talent, you should go for it. But don't think it's going to be easy. It's Hard!" **Aaliyah**

"Build business do for self" **Marcus Garvey**

"From the first time someone says, who do you think you are? We learn to repress." **Lauryn Hill**

"If you can't fly run, if you can't run walk, if you can't walk crawl. But by all means keep moving." **Martin Luther King JR.**

"All great achievements require time." **Maya Angelou**

"IT IS EASIER TO BUILD STRONG CHILDREN THEN TO REPAIR BROKEN MEN." **Frederick Douglas**

"There is always something to do. There are hungry people to feed, naked people to clothe, sick people to comfort and make well. And while

I don't expect you to save the world I do think it's not asking too much for you to love those with whom you sleep, share the happiness of those whom you call friend, engage those among you who are visionary and remove from your life those who offer you depression, despair and disrespect." **Nikki Giovanni**

"Believe in yourself. Take advantage of every opportunity. Use the power of spoken and written language to effect positive change for yourself and society." **Frederick Douglas**

"I freed a thousand slaves. I would have freed a thousand more if only they knew they were slaves." **Harriet Tubman**

"I you're white and your wrong, then your wrong: If you're black and you're wrong, you're wrong. People are people. Black, blue, pink, green- God makes no rules about color; only society makes rules where my people suffer, and that why we must have redemption and redemption now." **Bob Marley**

"Service is the rent you pay for room on this earth." **Shirley Chisholm**

"A society that keeps cures a secret so they can continue to sell medication for huge profits is not a real society but a huge mental asylum" **Dr. Sebi**

"Don't believe everything you hear. Real eyes, realize, real lies." **TUPAC**

"Segregation is wrong when it is forced by white people, and I believe it is still wrong when it is requested by black people." **Coretta Scott King**

"He who is not courageous enough to take risk will accomplish nothing in life." **Muhammad Ali**

"I will not rest until black children are taught to love themselves." **Dr. Frances Cress Welsing**

"Be to yourself stay to yourself, trust nobody trust nobody!" **Tupac**

"You wanna fly, you got to give up the shit that weights you down" **Toni Morrison**

I am a black American, I am proud of my race. I am proud of who I am. I have a lot of pride and dignity." **Michael Jackson**

"Trust yourself. Think of yourself. Act for yourself. Speak for yourself. Be yourself. Imitation is suicide." **Marva Collins**

George Washington Carvers eight cardinal Virtues
:Be clean both inside and out
; Neither looks up to the rich nor down to the poor
: Lose, if need be, without squealing
: Win without bragging
: Always be considerate of woman, children, and older people
: Be too brave to lie
: Be too generous to cheat
: Take your share of the world and let others take theirs

"No person is your friend who demands your silence, or denies your right to grow." **Alice Walker**

"Nobody said you have to be gangstas and hoes. Read more. Learn more. Change the Globe." **NAS**

"Just remember the world is not a playground but a schoolroom. Life is not a holiday but an education. One eternal lesson for us for all: to teach us how better we should love." **Barbara Jordan**

"Every human being has genius level talent, there's no chosen one God has given every single person genius level talent, you just have to find what it is that you are great at and then tap into it." **JAY Z**

"One chance is all you need." **Jesse Owens**

"If I don't love myself, I won't survive." **Lisa "Left Eye" Lopez**

"Every defeat, every heartbreak, every loss, contains its own seed. Its own lesson on how to improve your performance the next time." **Malcolm X**

"A lot of people don't know their purpose and if you don't know your purpose your immediate goal is to figure that out cause otherwise your just wondering around here, so the moment you can figure out what is your supposed to be doing the sooner you are able to get about the business of doing that." **Oprah**

"A spark can become a flame and change everything." **E.D. Nixon**

"In a world filled with hate we must still dare to hope in a world filled with anger we must still dare to comfort in a world filled with despair we must still dare to dream in a world filled with distrust we must still dare to believe." **Michael Jackson**

"What you learned, how you carried yourself, and how you'll be remembered is what matters." **Angie Martinez**

"When I say the word "Nigga" there's niggas and bitches that exist out here and you should call them as such. But it shouldn't be a descriptor of our people it should be a descriptor of ignorant people of all colors." **David Banner**

"When we start separating ourselves from our truths that's then when we start living in the dark just like a snake between two bricks but when we lift ourselves up and allow ourselves to be true to ourselves enough to say I'm hurt I'm broken I'm happy I'm sad that's when were able to be conscious in each moment and make the decisions to manifest the type of realities we want." **KeKe Palmer**

"I'm not going to stand up to show pride in a flag for a country that oppresses black people and people of color, to me, this is bigger than football and it would be selfish on my part to look the other way. There are bodies in the street and people getting paid leave and getting away with murder." **Colin Kaepernick**

"It was beautiful that I could represent those darker chocolate girls that don't always see themselves on the national stage." **Deshauna Barber**

"If you can see it in your head if you picture it if it's clear than it's a possibility. If you believe in it its already happed you just haven't gotten there yet. You have to learn how to recognize things you have to know what roads to take to get to your final destination because a thought just a thought form can manifest itself into a physical form it's all about believing in yourself believing what you do being able to see it knowing how to get there and living it." **Lisa "left eye" Lopez**

"Fellow citizens, pardon me, and allow me to ask. Why am I called upon to speak here today? What have I represent to do with your natural independence? Are the great principles of political freedom and of natural justice, embodied in that Declaration of Independence, extended to us? And am I, therefore, called upon to bring our humble offering to the national alter and to confess the benefits and express devout gratitude for the blessings resulting from your independence to us? Would to God both for your sakes and ours that an affirmative answer could be truthfully returned to these questions then would my task be light and my burden easy and delightful. For who is there so cold that a nations sympathy could not warm him? Who so obstruct and dead to the claims of gratitude that would not thankfully acknowledge such priceless benefits? Who so stoiled and selfish that would not give his voice to swell hallelujahs of a nations jubilee when the chains of servitude had been torn from his limbs? I am not that man in a case like that the dumb might eloquently speak and the lame man leap as a heart. But such is not the state of the case I say it with a sad sense of disparity between us. I am not included with the pale of this glorious anniversary. Your high independence only reveals the immeasurable distance between us." **Frederick Douglas** (What to a slave is Fourth of July 5 1852 Speech)

"If really is about networking across like who's next to you who's struggling who's in the trenches with you who's just as hungry as you are and those are the people that you need to build with…it's just about I guess passion and hunger."

Issa Rae

"Negros sweet and dolcile, meek, humble and kind. Beware the day they change their mind."
Langston Hughes

"it's a shame when niggas gone realize we the same you helping the enemy win the game if you a playa use precision Don't make a decision in haste your blood is a terrible thing to waste."
Goodie Mob

"The rich rob the poor and the poor rob one another." **Sojourner Truth**

"I'll never regret my silence. I will never regret my silence. Some people you can't talk too once I feel the energy I give everyone a change but once you come at me left then my perception of you has changed for life because u didn't have to do what you did me and you know I'm one hundred but you did that…but once you show me that you not one hundred after that its nothing…ill speak if you speak first…after that its nothing cause you showed me who you was."

Kevin Gates

"Nothing so frightens me as writing, but nothing so satisfies me. It's like a swimmer in the English Channel: you face the stingrays and waves and cold and grease, and finally you reach the other shore, and you put your foot on the ground-Aaaahhhh!" **Maya Angelou**

"Life is not one big road with lots of signs. So when you're riding through the ruts. Don't complicate your mind. Flee from hate, mischief and jealousy. Don't bury your thoughts. Put your vision to reality. Wake up and live." **Bob Marley**

"Just because I have my standards they think I'm a bitch." **Diana Ross**

"If we as people realized the greatness from which we came we would be less likely to disrespect ourselves." **Marcus Garvey**

"Those of us who stand outside the circle of this society's definition of acceptable woman: those of us who have been forged in the crucibles of difference – those of us who are poor, who are lesbians, who are Black, who are older – know that survival is not an academic skill. It is learning how to take our differences and make them strengths. For the masters tool will never dismantle the masters house. They may allow us temporarily to beat him at his own game, but they will never enable us to bring about genuine change. And this fact is only threatening to those women who still define the masters house as their only source of support." **Audre Lorde**

"Awards become corroded, friends gather no dust." **Jesse Owens**

"If there had not been a Claudette Colvin who did what Claudette Colvin did, then a lot of other events would not have occurred, it was a matter of each one building upon each other, and the rest is history." **Fred David Gray**

"I'll tell you what freedom is to me. No fear." **Nina Simone**

"I'm for truth no matter who tells it. I'm for justice no matter who it is for or against. I'm a human being first and foremost and as such I'm for whoever and whatever benefits humanity as a whole." **Malcolm X**

People look at me and think I should have and had everything I wanted. I'm one of the saddest people I know.
I'm motivated but I'm not pushed
I'm loved but nobodies in love with me
I'm young but I'm old I'm here and I'm alone.
These are the things that people envy me for
Isn't that funny,
because I have nothing that they don't have
I have exactly what everyone has.
So don't look at me and see better look at me and see you.
Don't tell me your issues because I'm cool and you know I can keep a secret tell me your issues because you trust me and you love me and you care.
I wish people really see me for me and not that picture they had in their mind from when I was younger.
we all know time changes everything
and it's been a long time since I been a child.
Do you know me or do you know who I used to

be
did you ever know me or did you know what I look like
would you ever know me or would you always know my past never my present?
When you look at me what do you see do you see somebody you envy or do you see somebody who's envious?
cause I know me and yes I know you too
I listen and watch, you've told me a thousand stories about you but notice I'm never broke down and talk to you like you talk to me
you don't know my deeps you don't know my outs you just know a few of my where and been a bouts
but I want you to know me and not that fictitious character
I want you to know the real this stuff that's running through my blood
my character
wish you knew me
cause your thought of me is not true
your expectations of me is not fair
the way you look at me I got thousand looks that give me the same stare they don't know me but they claim they do
I wish they did cause I could cry on them like they cry on me
it's always what they intend to do

and that's fine cause I take it all in and relieve them of that
I give them encouraging words just for them to leave me the hate and worry they just carried on their back
now I got to re-up because in their eyes it's easy for me to do
go listen to some music relieve release the pain
just to suck up a little bit more juice
so when you see me do you see you
or when you see me do you see a doormat for you
cause in your eyes
I'm spoiled I got it better than you
but in my eyes
I'm just me wishing and hoping
I could do, feel, and know few of the things that you go through.
Netta B.

"We all have dreams. In order to make dreams come into reality, it takes an awful lot of determination, dedication, self-discipline and effort." **Jessie Owens**

"It's time for you to move, realizing that the thing you are seeking is also seeking you." **Iyanla**

Vanzant

"If Hip Hop has the ability to corrupt young minds, it also has the ability to uplift them!" **KRS ONE**

"Nothing will work unless you do." **Maya Angelou**

"When I saved my 13th aids patient my mother said they are going to get you." **Dr. Sebi**

"You cannot continue to move forward in your life to the level and level and level that you need to be if you're surrounded by energy that brings you down that sucks the life force from you. You're not only responsible for the energy you bring your also responsible for the energy you surround yourself with." **Oprah**

"If there is no struggle, there is no progress" Frederick Douglass
"Have a vision. Be demanding." **Colin Powell**

"What difference does it make if the thing you are scared of is real or not?" **Toni Morrison**

"Africans did not come over here as Niggas that was a program. We have been programed black folks don't even know why they hate themselves like they do they hate themselves because they've been program to want to be a white person and people distained the fact they can't grow their hair like you…You are killing them just by existing." **David Banner**

"the most potent weapon in the hands of the oppressor is the mind of the oppressed" **Bantu Stephen Biko**

Angry I'm angry
I'm mad thinking about all the things I've could have had
I'm thinking about opportunities
I'm thinking about circumstances
I thinking about one in lifetime chances
I passed up because I was mad
Now I'm angry
I think about the people that I've met

The places that I've been
The conversations that I've had
The money that I would just spend
and I'm mad I'm angry
I sit back and think how do you push so many people away
How do you spend so much money in day
How could you let such a good thing go away
did you miss out
Is there never going to be another change
was it for your better
Were you not supposed to move duck and dodge
Did you actually do what you were supposed to do
Is it true you dodge bullets from a concealed position
Not knowing you were positioning
yourself
I missed out on opportunities
I missed out on relationships
I missed out on it all
Because I was mad I was angry
But now I see a better picture
I see a bigger picture
I see everything happening for the picture
Now I'm going after everything that I missed out on
Now any opportunity that presents itself is a strike out because I'm mad I'm angry"

Netta B.

"love so tried but true been broken but you still came through
"I have fought against White domination and I have fought against black domination. I have cherished the ideal of a democratic and free society in which all persons will live together in harmony and with equal opportunities. It is an ideal which I hope to live for and to see realized. But if it needs be, it is an ideal for which I am prepared to die." **Mandela's Rivonia Trial Speech 1964**

"I've failed over and over and over again in my life. And that's why I succeed." **Michael Jordan**

"Musicians that are true to themselves no matter how big your platform or how bright your spotlight…it's because of you that the world goes round…don't be fooled, be you and don't let anybody infiltrate your dream and make sure you saying something when you saying something it is important to sound like you to feel like you to be like you." **Erykah Badu**

"You have to have such a strong belief of yourself that you can quiet out all the outside noise and you're going to need that every step of the way there are people that are projecting their fears or shortcomings and failures on you and you have to be very careful about that" **JayZ**

"Sometimes it is worst to win a fight than to lose." **Billie Holiday**

"When you do the common things in life in an uncommon way, you will command the attention of the world." **George Washington Carver**

"Be thankful for what you have: you'll end up having more. If you concentrate on what you don't have, you will never, ever have enough." **Oprah Winfrey**

"I'd always end up broken down on the highway. When I stood there trying to flag someone down, nobody stopped. But when I pushed my own car, other drivers would get out and push with me. If you want help, help yourself!" **Chris Rock**

"And he said: You pretty full of yourself ain't you? So she replied: Show me someone not full of herself and I'll show you a hungry person." **Nikki Giovanni**

"in 1860 99% of all black people worked for whites. Today, 98% of all blacks works for whites. Are you enjoying a social illusion because you go to someone else's restaurant, but you don't own the restaurant yourself." **Dr. Claud Anderson**

"Success is liking yourself, liking what you do, and liking how you do it." **Maya Angelou**

"The most revolutionary thing a Black man can do, living in a racist society, is to love, respect, and protect his Black woman." **Minister Tony Bradford**

"Write it down on real paper with a real pencil and watch shit get real" **Erykah Badu**

"My advice to anyone looking to start a business is be fearless believe in the impossible and dream like a kid." **Mikaila Ulmer**

"I'm only nineteen but my minds old, when things get treal my warm heart turns cold another nigga deceased, another story gets told it ain't nothing really, ayo dun spar the Philly." **MOBB DEEP**

"Teach the youth feed the needy confident descendent of Nefertiti the mother of civilization will rise. Like the cream and still build the strong foundation secondary but necessary to reproduce acknowledged the fact that I'ma black and I don't lack" **Queen Latifah**

"Be rebellious and speak about it" **Prodigy**

"The more I follow politics the more I realize politicians just full of shit. Mf can just lie to you bout whatever they want to lie to you about and just keep it moving like it never even happen. I go to court right now they make me raise my hand and they swear me in…and if they catch me lying my ass is grass but not no politician. …And ain't no way a drug killer killing more than them but nothing can happen to a Politian they just kill you and play games with you and lie to you and everything supposed to be peaches and mf cream." **Plies**

"Don't be in such a hurry to condemn a person because he doesn't do what you do or think as you think. There was a time when you didn't know what you know today." **Malcolm X**

"I think I aspire people to do many things because when I was young and very impressable you know the arts that I loved inspired me just as I'm sure that I inspire young people and maybe even to be musicians and singers but mostly I want people to feel better by any means necessary and find their own space their own place in the world where they can grow and be free and learn from their mistakes and move on quickly." **Erykah Badu**

"We should emphasize not Negro History, but the negro in history. What we need is not a history of selected races or nations, but the history of the world void of national bias, race hate, and religious prejudice." **Carter Woodson on the subject of founding black history week**

"If you are silent about your pain they'll kill you and say you enjoyed it." **Zora Neale Hurston**

"A MF gone tell me: *Yeah, you know being dark skinned is a thing now.* I said *Bih you as dark as me and you talking about a thing now? You got to be bout twenty years my senior and talking bout a thing now!?* That was the perfect example of self-hate and influence." **Netta B.**

"The secret of life is to have no fear; it's the only way to function." **Stokely Carmichael**

"Not only the Negro child but children of all races should read and know of the achievements, accomplishments and deeds of the Negro. World peace and brotherhood are based on a common understanding of the contributions and cultures of all races and creeds." **Mary McLeod Bethune**

"...Let us not wallow in the valley of despair, I say to you today, my friends.
And so even though we face the difficulties of today and tomorrow, I still have a dream. It is a dream deeply rooted in the American dream.
I have a dream that one day this nation will rise up and live out the true meaning of its creed: "we hold these truths to be self-evident, that all men are created equal."
I have a dream that one day on the red hills of Georgia, the sons of former slaves and the sons of former slave owners will be able to sit down together at the table of brotherhood
I have a dream that one day even the state of Mississippi, a state sweltering with the heat of injustice, swelting with the heat of oppression, will be transformed into a oasis of freedom and justice.
I have a dream that my four little children will one day live in a nation where they will not be judged by the color of their skin but by the content of their character.
I have a dream today.
I have dream that one day, down in Alabama, with its vicious racist, with its governor having his lips dripping with the words of interposition and nullification...one day right there in Alabama little black boys and black girls will be able to join

hands with little white boys and white girls as sisters and brothers

I have a dream today

I have a dream that one day every valley shall be exalted, and every hill and mountain shall be made low, the rough places will be made plain, and the crooked places will be made straight and the glory of the lord shall be revealed and all flesh shall see it together.

This is our hope, and this is the faith that I go back to the south with.

With this faith, we will be able to hew out of the mountain of despair a stone of hope. With this faith, we will be able to transform the jangling discords of our nation into a beautiful symphony of brotherhood. With this faith, we will be able to work together, to pray together, to struggle together, to go jail together, to stand up for freedom together, knowing that we will be free one day.

….and if America is to be a great nation, this must be true.

…and when this happens, and when we allow freedom ring, when we let it ring from every village and every hamlet, from every state and every city, we will be able to speed up that day when all God's children, black men and white men, Jews and Gentiles, Protestants and Catholics, will be able to join hands and sing in the words of the old Negro spiritual, Free at last! Free at last! Thank God Almighty, we are free at last. **Martin Luther King Jr.**

"Let it (Racism) be a problem to someone else…Let it drag them down. Don't use it as a excuse for you own shortcomings." **Colin Powell**

"You must remain hungry and humble key words. Words to live by, you must remain hungry and humble! So you stay hungry you gotta stay on the gas pedal gotta stay all gas no brake pads and you gotta stay humble you can't get big headed start burning bridges high siding on people that helped you get to where you at… The OG's used to tell me when I was a young mustache get you a house own a piece of the earth…. It can be a fixer upper it don't have to be no mansion as long as you just got some property once you run across some extra dollars but get that before you get a $85,000 car." **E-40**

"A job is a hustle and a hustle is a job. Money never stops and determination never fails. We all got something we after, and a lot of shit good and bad came with a chase." **Netta Boo**

"Well they go down in history as just being athletes. I'm givin more and credit for what I'm just doing now on this show then beating the five-year English Champion Because right now black people when you show this show are home jumping home shouting because they don't have the nerve to say what I'm saying and nobody's never said it and their just so happy to see a black man who will stand up and jeopardize every quarter he's got to tell the truth… So like Floyd Patterson and other fighters they just don't take part they make him a millions dollars get him a rolls Royce get a nice home get him a white wife well I made it and Americas great and the rest of them catching hell and they won't say nothing... but when one man of popularity can let the world know the problem he may lose a few dollars himself telling the truth he may lose his life but he's helping millions but if I kept my mouth shut cause I can make millions then this ain't doing nothing I love the freedom and the flesh and blood of my people more so then I do the money." **Muhamed Ali**

"Every war has a casualty and any casualty can

cause a war." **Netta B.**

"I got to hustle for my own and any man out there got to feel me… I'm finna come up on my own… I don't wanna be nobodies worker all my life… aint no one man gone stay in one spot foreva." **Tupac**

"My granddaddy use to tell me you just like a lighter going bad people gotta be gentle but fast with you in order to get the flame. They gotta be fast because you don't play games you want the facts up front. What do they want from you? How will it benefit you? And gentle because you're a diamond your rare not many girls built like you. You are going to go through so much before you see your victory and baby girl your day will come as long as you stay true and focused to what you want." **Netta B.**

"I never watch what somebody else does it does not matter Bernie Mac gotta do his thing…to be the best within myself I'm not in competition with anybody…I think if you focus on being the best within yourself all that stuff will come. I hear people say get your money up get your money up I hate that…that's your motivation? If you do if you do well the money will come." **Bernie Mac**

"We are all gifted. That is our inheritance." **Ethel Waters**

"All things are possible who you are is limited by who you think you are." **Egyptian Book of the Dead**

"Want for your brother what you want for yourself." **Prophet Muhommad**

"I stay true to myself and my style and I am always pushing myself to be aware of that and be original." **Aaliyah**

"No living white person is responsible for slavery at all but all living whites reap it's benefits, just like all living blacks wear its scars." **Talib Kweli**

"When there is no enemy within, the enemies outside cannot hurt you." **African Proverb**

I am defiant if I SEPARATE
I am fake if I ASSIMILATE
They consider my uniqueness STRANGE
They call my language SLANG
They see my confidence as CONCEIT
They see my mistakes as DEFEAT
My questions mean I am UNAWARE
My advancement is somehow UNFAIR
To voice concern is DISCONTENTMENT
If I stand up for myself I am to DEFENSIVE
If I don't trust them I am too APPERHENSIVE
They consider my success ACCIDENTAL
They minimize my intelligence to POTENTIAL
They take my kindness for WEAKNESS
They take my silence for SPEECHLESS
My character is constantly UNDERRATTED
Pride for my race makes me TOO BLACK
Nijia Candy

"I pray God will bless you in everything that you do. I pray that you will grow intellectually so that you can understand the problems of the world and were you fit into in that world picture and I pray all the fear in your heart will be taken out." **Malcolm X**

The best Quote of 2017: *"I'm reclaiming my time"* **Maxine Waters** Every Black person should be screaming this this! We still got time to get it together.

"Melanin a curse in a blessing, but a curse is just a mind thing." **Netta B**

"What are you talking about? Just do it, that's all you have to do Netta."

MA

MELANIN PLAYLIST

Do you really listen to the words of the music? Music is not always about the turn up. Music derived from a form of expression, music derived from a form of celebration, music derived from a form of mourning. Every song every note is meant to express a form of a emotion, every song that's written is formed to relay a message, every song that is wrote is usually for the better but sometimes you really have to listen to what message your bobbing your head to. You have to hear the words that are being said you have to choose what you allow into your body your mind because all music is not good music. Music was originally made to relay a message to speak you have to stop praising what's just a beat basically with two or good punch lines or word play and saying the single is fire and really seek some music that feeds the soul and your mind. Music that pushes, progresses, excites you, music is life as far as I'm concerned music does something for me and it always has, and music has always been my release factor and always will be so I can genuinely understand or feel an artist. Erykah Badu's Love of My Life is my music ode too. Lol. Music movies books it's all a form of truth even though it's over a beat made to entertain and make you jovial it is all a message an expression, a truth, at least that's what it is supposed to be you got to know what you vouching for.

"Don't just listen to the beat hear the words. Music is the key to any and everyone's soul. The stories and feelings of everyday people, it has always been our communication."
Netta B

"Wisdom in rap, You can educate your people from the enemy with just one rap... one rap is worth one hundred sermons."

Louis Farrakhan

"Music is my heart and soul it's more precious than gold" Marvin Gaye

Marvin Gaye- Just Like Music *(Music Fill the Soul* **1978)**
Eric Sermon ft. Marvin Gaye- Music (2001)

FEEL GOOD (let it go)

Sounds of Blackness- Optimistic (1991) Hold On *Change Is Comin'* (1991)
Marvin Gaye- Trouble Man, Mercy Mercy Me (1971)
Bill Withers- Lovely Day, (1977)
Staple Singers- Let's do it Again (1975), I'll Take You There (1972)
T.K. Soul- Party Like Back in the Day (2007)
Sir Charles Jones- Friday (2008)
Mary J. Blige- Just Fine (2007) Work That (2007)
Childish Gambino- Redbone (2017)
Whitney Houston & CeCe Winans- Count On Me (1995
Maze- Happy Feelings (1977)
Aretha Franklin- A Rose is Still a Rose (1998)
Lauryn Hill- Everything Is Everything (1998)
Sam Cooke- A Change is Gonna Come (1964) Having a Party (1962)
Louis Armstrong- What a Wonderful World (1967)
Ben E King- Stand by Me (1962)
Erykah Badu- On & On (1997)
Dionne Warwick- That's what Friends Are For (1985)
Beyoncé- Formation (2016)
Michael Jackson- They Don't Care About Us (1995)
India Arie- Beautiful Flower (2009) I Am Not My Hair *ft. AKON* (2006)
Stevie wonder- I Wish (1976)
Jill Scott- Hate on Me (2007)
Arrested Development- People Everyday (1992)
Lucy Pearl- Dance Tonight (2000)
Sly & The Family Stone- Everyday People (1969) Thank You (1969)
James Brown- Say it Loud, I'm Black and I'm Proud (1968)

Koffee Brown- After Party (2001)
Akon- Pot of Gold (2005)
The O'Jays- Love Train (1972)
Goapele- Closer (2001)
Donny Hathaway- The Ghetto (1970)

RAP

DJ Premier featuring Rakim, NAS, KRS-One- Classic (2007)
Nas- Street Dreams (1996) One Mic (2001), I Can (2002), If I Ruled the World (1996)
Jada kiss: Why (2004)
Tupac and Scarface- Smile (1996)
MC Lyte- Paper Thin (1988), Poor Georgie (1991) Keep On Keepin On (1996)
DMX- Slippin (1998)
Trick Daddy- Thug Holiday (2002)
The Sugar Hill Gang- Rappers Delight (1979) *1ST RAP SONG EVER RECORDED*
Ice Cube- It was a Good Day (1990), It Takes a Nation (2008)
2PAC- Changes (1992), Only God Can Judge Me (1996), All Eyez On Me (1996), Keep Ya Head Up (1993)
Lupe Fiasco- Bad Bitch (2012)
Roxanne Shante- Roxanne's Revenge (1985) Have a Nice Day (1989)
Funkadelic- One Nation Under a Groove (1978)
Grandmaster Flash & The Furious Five- The Message (1982)
Akon ft. Styles P- Locked Up (2004)
KRS-One- Sound of the Police (1993) MC's Act Like

MELANIN

They Don't Know (1995)
Lauryn Hill- Doo Wop *That Thing* (1998)
Rakim- The Mystery (1997) Holy Are You (2009)
Dj Khaled- Never Surrender (2013)
2Pac- Keep Ya Head Up (1993)
Public Enemy- Fight The Power (1990)
Boosie Badazz- Wake Up (2016) Show da World (2014)
Mos Def- Mathematics (1999)
Coolio- Gangsta Paradise (1995)
Dj Kool Herc- Let Me Clear My Throat (1996)
Jay Z- The Story of O.J. (2017)
Goodie Mob- The Experience (1998), Beautiful Skin (1998) Get up, Get out
Queen Latifah- Just Another Day (1993) U.N.I.T.Y (1994)
Salt N Pepa- Let's Talk About Sex (1990)

LOVE

Luther Vandross and Cheryl Lynn- If This World Were Mine (1982)
Bill Withers- Grandma Hands (1971)
Michael Jackson- The Way You Make Me Feel (1987), Remember the Time (1991)
Al Green- Lets Stay Together (1972)
Marvin Gaye and Tammi Terrell- Your All I Need (1968)
Akon- Don't Matter (2007)
Betty Wright- No Pain, No Gain (1988)
Chaka Khan- Tell Me, (1974) Sweet Thing (1975)
Erykah Badu- Otherside of the Game (1997)
Angie Stone-Brotha (2001)
India Arie- Brown Skin (2001) Chocolate High featuring

Netta B.

Musiq Soulchild (2009) Talk to Her (2002)
Truth (2002)
Whitney Houston- I Believe In You And Me (1996)
Stevie Wonder- Signed, Sealed, Delivered (1970)
Erykah Badu ft. Stephen Marley- In Love with You (2002)
Bill Withers- Just the Two of Us (1980)
Calvin Richardson and Angie Stone- More Than a Woman (2002)
Jill Scott and Anthony Hamilton- So in Love (2011)
Peaches and Herb- Reunited (1978)
Sade- Your Love Is King (1984)
Stevie Wonder-My Cherie Amour (1969)
Luther Vandross- Always and Forever (1994) Here and Now (1989) Take You Out (2001)
Anthony Hamilton- Point of It All (2008) Cool (2008)
Bobby Caldwell- What You Won't Do For Love (1978)

BONUS

Common ft. Mary J. Blige- Come Close (2002)
Mary J. Blige and Method Man- Your All I Need (1995)

REGAE

Baby Cham ft. Alicia Keys- Ghetto Story (2006)
Mr. Vegas- I am Blessed (2012)
Bob Marley- Redemption song (1980)
Tory Lanez- Controlla (2016)
I-Wayne- Cant Satisfy Her (2005)
Tanta Metro and Devonte- Everyone Falls In Love Sometimes (1999)
Sean Paul- Still in love with you (2002)
Chaka Demus & Pliers- Murder She Wrote (2011)

Serani- No Games (2009)
T.O.K. - Footprints (2005)
Kranium- Nobody Has to Know (2015)
Wayne Wonder- No Letting Go (2003)
Gyptian- Non Stop (2013)
Mavado- I'm So Special (2011)
Patra
Mad Cobra- Flex (1992)
Rupee- Tempted 2 Touch (2004)
Pressure- Love and Affection (2007)
Future Fambo- Rum and Redbull (2011)
Damian Marley- Welcome to Jamrock (2005)

SPIRITUALS that held coded messages about escaping to north or the enslavement of Black people most of the below songs have a variety of versions.
Fisk Jubilee Singers- Motherless child/Sometimes I Feel Like a Motherless Child (1870's)
Fisk Jubilee Singers- Sweet Low, Sweet Chariot (1909)
Fisk Jubilee Singers- Wade in the Water (1901)
Fisk Jubilee Singers-Go Down Moses (1872)
Fisk Jubilee Singers- The Gospel Train (1872)
Fisk Jubilee Singers- Steal away (1862)
Thelma La Vizzo- I'm troubled in mind (1924)

RAG TIME, BLUES, and JAZZ

B.B King (Jazz)
Bessie smith (Blues)
Muddy waters (Blues)

Billy Holiday (Blues)
Ma Rainey (Blues)
Nina Simone (Jazz/Blues)
Sister Rosetta Tharpe (Rock & Roll/Gospel)
Ethel waters (Jazz)
Lester young (Jazz)
Miles Davis (Jazz)
Coon song (Rag time)
Cake walk
Scott Joplin- Maple Leaf Rag (Ragtime 1899)

GOSPEL

Various Artist- Father Can You Hear Me (2005)
Tata Vega- God Is Trying To Tell You Something (1986)
Mahalia Jackson- His Eye Is On the sparrow (1905)
Shirley Caesar- No Charge (1987)
Smokie Norful- I Need You Now (2002)
Anita Baker & The Winans- Ain't No Need to Worry (1988)
Fred Hammond- No Weapon (1998)
Thomas Dorsey- It's a Highway to Heaven (1973)
Timothy Wright- Trouble Don't Last Always (1991)
Tamela Mann- Take Me to the King (2012)
Dixie hummingbirds- Amazing Grace (1946)
DeWayne Woods- Let Go (2007)
Yolanda Adams- The battle is the Lords (1993)
Clara Ward Singers- How I Got Ova (1951)
The Rance Allen Group ft. Kirk Franklin- Something About the Name Jesus (2007)
Rev. Paul Jones- I won't Complain (1993)
Hezekiah Walker- I Need You to Survive (2002)

MELANIN

Kirk Franklin- The storm is over now (1997)
Mary Mary- God in me (2008) Go Get It (2012)
Donnie McClurkin- We Fall Down (2002)
Marvin Sapp- Never Would of Made It (2007)
BeBe & CeCe Winans- Addictive Love (1991) Close to You (2009)
Byron Cage- Shabach (2001)
Mahalia Jackson- We Shall Overcome (originally made by Charles Albert Tindley "I SHALL OVERCOME" in 1900)

R.I.P

Boyz II Men- It's So Hard to Say Goodbye to Yesterday (1991)
Mariah Carey & Boyz II Men- One Sweet Day (1995)
Jamie Foxx- I Wish You Were Here (2005)
Luther Vandross- Dance with My Father (2003)
Immature- Alone (1997)
Dianna Ross- Missing You (1989)
D.R.S. - Gangsta Lean (1993)
Aaliyah- I Miss You (2001)
Bones Thugs N Harmony- Crossroads (1995)
2Pac- I Ain't Mad at Cha (1996)
Brandy, Tamia, Gladys Knight, Chaka Khan- Missing You (1996)
Kanye West- Coldest Winter (2008)
Craig David- Let Her Go (2005)
Sean Combs ft. Faith Evans & 112- I'll be missing you (1997)
Lost Boyz- Renee (1996)

Netta B.

Master P- Goodbye To My Homies (1998)
Wu-Tang Clan- Life Changes (2007)
The Game, Chris Brown, Diddy, Mario Winans, Polow Da Don, Usher, Boyz II Men- Better On The Other Side (2009)
Pete Rock and CL Smooth- They Reminisce Over You *T.R.O.Y* (1992)
Smokey Robinson- Really Gonna Miss You (2005)
Mariah Carey- Bye Bye (2008)
Kandi- Easier (2000)

Wake Up Young World (Bonus Tracks)

Stop the Violence Movement- Self Destruction (1988)
Nina Simone- Why *The King of Love Is Dead* (1968)
Stevie Wonder- Higher Ground (1973) Living for the City (1973)
Marvin Gaye- What's Going On (1971) Inner City Blues *Makes Me Wanna Holla* (1971)
Harold and the Blue notes ft. Teddy Pendergrass- Wake Up Everybody (1975)
Curtis Mayfield- Move on Up (1970)
William DeVaughn- Be Thankful For What You Got (1974)
Stephanie Mills- Home (1989)
Groove Theory- Keep Tryin' (1995)
Earth, Wind, and Fire- That's the Way of The World (1975)
Keni Burke- Risin' to the Top (1982)
Gil Scott-Heron- The Revolution Will Not Be Televised (1970)

MAZE ft. Frankie Beverly- We Are One (1983)
Childish Gambino- Redbone

When the World Is All On One Tune
**U.S.A. For Africa- We Are the World (1985)
We Are the World 25 for Haiti (2010)**

In the music industry it seems like all the rappers that are making it big are really young barely out of the high school doors and these kids probably haven't really ever had much, feel like they have to prove they have street cred, they lost. My point is the new young aged leaders in the media still have to learn themselves so that's what they are doing they're learning. The only difference is they are doing it with stacks of money under the cameras and with a very limited amount of real friends if any. The perfect mix for self-destruction for them-selves and the youth following or looking up to them. The best thing to do is take them for what they are entertainers not role models.

Race records: records made for the black consumer containing different genres i.e. jazz, gospel, blues and comedy in the 1921-1942 after World War II Rhythm and Blues replaced it.

WERD was the first African American operated and owned radio station produced in Atlanta Georgia

Netta B.

October 3 1949 Jesse B. Blayton

BET (Black Entertainment Television) first African American oriented cable network established 1980
RAP CITY: premiered August 11, 1989

The media and music are the world's main influence of today. What we live off of and is inspired and provoked very heavily influenced by today. What they lacked back in the day they gained from music they created back in the day. Music, hymns, chants, beats (instruments) were their motivation during slavery times music was used to communicate or just get someone through the day of the manual labor banjo came to the states from Africans and drums also, but drums were later banned on plantations because slave owners later found out drums were being used as a form of communication. Sometimes slave owners and family would sit and enjoy the music of slaves made by their makeshift instruments, body parts, and fiddles singing or hymning their gospel, blues, or spirituals. That form of music became known as blue grass or country music.
The media is feeding everyone bullshit! Television is a mockery of the black race and black family's or lack thereof. Music is becoming a joke there is no unity no real family reunion music. Remember when you could play whatever came on the radio at a cookout or whatever and just vibe? Now everything has to be censored and what is not censored should probably be.
I've always wondered how a person can get so hype to a song at any given moment in the club specifically to

where they think that song is narrating their life at the specific moment in time that they get so hype and cranked up. I chuckle then move away, lol. No but seriously how does music get somebody in such a trance to where they block reality or consequences? Or is it to where they just feel that beat with life and reality? Some music can make you want to give up or not care, yall better start filtering this shit coming on the radio. We have to remember that whenever we hear music 99.9 percent of the time it is just used to set a mood, get that mood going to wherever or whatever environment. Whether it is at the club, a lounge with a live band, a restaurant or elevator a mood is being set for that environment, mood, surroundings or actions taking place. It's all serving a purpose…to calm you, living you up, to place in a mood to enjoy, praise, reflect, or relax. That's it. It's not an instruction manual but a free therapy session.

Did you know that on June 7, 1979 President Jimmy Carter declared June be the month of black music?

I found this on one of those social sites this meaning of the acronym of **HIP HOP: High Infinite Power Healing Our People**. (I thought that's nice.) MAYBE because that's what music use to really be about feeling good or true mood expression not attempting to be better or tougher.

Rap Artist as early as the 1980's- 1990's have been linked to the Five Percenters and known for **"Droppin Science!"**

"With black music, jazz music, the blues, with hip hop, its art that is mandatory. It's a natural resource...Its connected to the culture." Talib Kweli

"The Industry man it's not the same, doesn't have to do with talent it's about playing a game. The Industry REAL NEGUS is dying to get in, the Industry just to find they don't fit in. The Industry aint what it used to be, The Industry tryna control the way you MC. They want to dress like this and talk like that but I'm gone dress like this and talk with the bat. The Industry that's your word meaning nothing The Industry fuck what you heard cause he bluffin the industry money bitches hate but I dare you to try to take a fuckin thing off my plate The Industry like wait, but in the streets we like get em seventeen up in that thing catch em sleepin hit em. The Industry if don't got a strong mind, The Industry will break you down it's a matter of time." DMX

"Hip Hop can be a very powerful weapon to help expand young peoples' political and social consciousness. But just as with any weapon, if you don't know how to use it, if you don't know where to point it, or what you're using it for,

MELANIN

you can end up shooting yourself in the foot or killing your sisters or brothers."

Assata Shakur

Netta B.

MOMENT OF SILENCE

#Sandra Bland

#Wayne Jones

#Jimmie Lee Jackson

#Mary Turner

#Kathryn Johnston

#Alton Sterlings

#Keiauna Davis

#Ashawnty Davis

#Dr. Sebi

Netta B.

#Bianca Nikol Roberson

#Bakari Henderson

#Prince

#Jordan Edwards

#Kerrice Lewis

#Sean Suiter

#Charles Eddie Moore

#Henry Hezekiah Dee

#Trayvon Martin

#Kiwane Carrington

#Malcom X

#Kimberlee-Randle King

#Stephon Alonzo Clark

#Ashley Francois

#Johnny Robinson (1963)

#Kalief Browder

#Kendra Jones

MELANIN

#Pvt. Emmanuel Mensah

#Michael Jackson

#Whitney Houstan

#Victor White

#Marielle Franco

#Emmett Till

#Mark Clark (activist)

#Kalief browder

#Glenn Ford

#Chavis Carter

#Amadou Diallo

#Bianca Nikol Roberson

#Dione Payne

#Alfred Wright

#Dr. Delbert Blair

#Gabriel Taye

#L. Alex Wilson

Netta B.

#Charleena Lyles

#Louis Allen

#Symone Marshall

#Renisha McB

#Edson

#Malissa Williams

#James Byrd Jr.

#Hazel "Hayes" Turner

#Jermaine Baker

#Sarah Reed

#Derek Williams (2011)

#Mark Duggan

#Kenneka Jenkins

#Terence Crutcher

#Michael Donald

#Laura Nelson

#Roger Sylvester

MELANIN

#Joy Gardner

#Tommy Le

#Korryn Gaines

#John Crawford III

#Richard Collins III

#Kendra James

#Muammar Gaddafi

#Makeva Jenkins

#Drekia Boyd

#Jordan Edwards

#Sam Cooke

#India Kager

#Michael Brown

#DeAndre Joshua

#The little rock nine

#Sept15 1963

#Yvette Smith

Netta B.

#Fred Hammond

The foul fourteen

#Dawon Gore

#Christopher Middleton

#Shareese Francis

#Miriam Carey

#Phillip White

#Miosotis Familia

#Dymond Milburn

#Prince

#Latasha Harlins

#Martin Luther King Jr.

#LaVena Johnson

#Quintonio LeGrier

#Alesia Thomas

#Tupac

#Eric Garner

MELANIN

#Malissa Williams

#Alfred Wright

#Philandro Castile

#Gynnya McMillen

#Sean Bell

#Shantel Davis

#Tamir Rice

#Medgar Wiley Evers

#Sam Dubose

#Oscar Grant

#Aiyana Stanley Jones

#Chavis Carter

#Troy Anthony Davis

#Haile Clacken

#Emidio Josias Mido Macia

#Andrea Heath

#Nabra Hassanen

"I'd like to say sorry to the families of Aiyana Jones, Michael Brown, Eric Garner and I want to apologize for them for not being able to get justice for their love ones who were murdered in cold blood and on respect for the peaceful protest I want to say hand up, don't shoot, black lives matter. That's all your honor." Frederick Young

"Those who commit the murders write the reports."

Ida B. Wells

MELANIN

FINAL THOUGHTS

In order to have better descendants and your very own bright future we have to check ourselves and be mindful of the kids and children around us. Sometimes kids don't need to hear everything see or have opinions to every or any adult conversation neither do they always need to be sitting under them.

When we think about our "friends" our "homies" we need to really sit and think about who we give these titles to. When you think back in history, think about all the people that have done good for humanity who put confidence, knowledge, determination, good spirit, and health in people. These people are often assassinated. Really think about how these people died I mean perfect or close to perfect health just die. Please do asset what's going on around you and don't always just take the words of others. When you hanging with your "friend" and they bring a "friend" do you just assume they are cool because they are with your friend or do watch listen and decide.

Eight times out of the ten, people are assassinated/murdered with the help or by someone they know being behind it, it is someone who knows or has access to your pattern. People are so into themselves and what the status is, it's mainly all about what they have to be and none of what they have to do. I have be flyy, I gotta be a bad bitch, I have be mean, I have to be there. I rarely hear I have to go to work, I have to finish this goal,

I have to read that book, I have to watch out for them.
Everybody so worried about being recognized they can't even see the snakes the wolves or even the angel's and helpers because they mixing the two together and at the end of the day making a fail for self because you are all about you. It is nothing wrong with being all about you, you are supposed to be all about you but you are not supposed to be on some I gotta doodoo on this person today or tomorrow. That's not how you progress not by shittin on people not making fake façade's about yourself just to have people believe something that's not even true. Cause now you about to kill yourself to keep that image up. Why you even started that? There was no need. All you have to do is be yourself and somebody is going to flock to you. Be yourself and the person that you want or the person that you need is going to flock to you, instead of the person that you don't need and you might not even know. They might have all of everything but they still want more so now you are they prey, now it's what can they get out of you and once they realize you not what they thought you was, your gone, your services are no longer for them or needed by them. And I guess you can say that's life.

Be mindful be in the know open your eyes see almost everything is a facade you can see the truth if you open your eyes but mostly everything is a facade. Everything that's neat everything that's pretty everything that's low-key that's where some of the most dangerous people go, Why? Because aint no police, it aint hot, aint no heat you really have to evaluate people by their mind by their actions you cannot depend on words because now a days it is so easy for somebody to tell a lie. Words are minute today. How many times somebody told you something and I don't know you really believed and thought it was truth only to realize not so much. I'm sure it was plenty of times but we have to realize that we gotta open our eyes start doing what is in our hearts and guts and stop going against the grain of thangs we are going to always fail if we go against the grain, if what you doing is ultimately for someone else rather than yourself. To be honest that's basically what media tells us to do is compete and we have to get that competitive spirit off of us. It is not about competing we really don't have to because it's so much money out here it's a broad ass place you don't have to just focus on your hood you could sell to any country you want to, the way technology is set up today and realistically be a millionaire in no time. Stop thinking about competing and just do your thing be true to self, money is going to come if you stop being so friendly and keeping these humongous circles or squads you could do some things. With that big click you got I'm sure things can get a little confusing or hectic so many people talking and opinions when low-key it's just a friendly competition.

We have to do better with kids we have to talk and teach and stop sitting these kids in front of televisions your letting somebody else raise your child. Whoever that someone else is the one that's putting whatever they want on the television on that particular station. Now you wondering why your child is like they are or have so much personality like dang how the heck they get so grown so quickly because it's your mouth and attitude plus the T.V. starting with the cartoons that's so deep and advanced it keeps adults interested like dang this little dog and cat or whatever got the mess going on, so if its keeping your grown behind attention imagine what it does to the kids. So that's why I say you can't let media raise your kids. Because it's not like the 80 early 90's television shows care bears rescue rangers Saturday morning cartoons kid approved television has evolved with the times and is not lagging. There is no more care or help someone figure out a problem help even your nemesis. Now it's just plan competition, selfishness, sneaky, and being deceiving and that's for every episode.

So we have to implement ourselves into these kids and teach them our heritage our culture those first two to three years are vital. Television and schools don't represent color like they should but in a negative light and the worst is they may even represent us with a white face and it's not fair or right. Think about how you were raised think about how the people older than you were raised now look and think about the people younger than you were raised compare the differences think about they particular struggle because everyone is a product of their environment think about what this book has brought to your attention and will continue to bring to your attention and put it together think about how motivated people were back in the day and when you read their individual stories a lot of these people hung out together or had passing a couple of times it goes to show the company you keep is imperative.

Think about how discouraged people were back in the day and think about why and then look at today think about did those discouragements those whipping those slavery days emancipation days did that make a particular person bitter or stronger? Think about did that person take it to their descendants what mood did they plant in that child's head what did they share and this is how you have some people that just don't want to hear nothing but white people are either good or bad no in between

Metaphorically speaking our life and the easiness of it or lack thereof, follow me now picture what I'm saying. Ok your walking strolling shooting the breeze then you come up on closed locked door your only route to proceed and you guessed it you don't have a key. Now you have to find out what the code is finally opening it a couple steps in, you stumble. Quickly catching your balance right before you missed a step unaware a staircase was immediately ahead you fall rolling down the stairs to the bottom the fall is over you dust yourself access the injuries and think about the causes of the fall so you can get back up to ground level. Life is full of fails and falls and just like when you were a baby you kept trying kept seeking and you grew daily. That's Life. I been speaking a lot about how one can make themselves better which is a course that ultimately has to be taken **I can't express enough how you can't help anyone until you can help yourself. After you help yourself then you venture into trying to uplift others and that's where we as a race come together it's time to rightfully claim and own a piece of the world instead of funding it.** Glimpsing through this book you know that it's not us that has the problem but others that have a problem with us. Why is this because they don't want us to believe, to know, to be, or to even love ourselves because those four attributes along with Unity makes us incredibly dangerous!

> *"Being hard is too hard, being easy better."* Netta B.

MELANIN

Netta B.

ANSWER KEY

All multiple choice answers are letter **C**.
All true and false answers are **True**.

Stay Woke: derived from the Ferguson situation; stay conscious of the apparatus of white supremacy, don't just accept media or official reasons or explanations for police violence. Be mindful, stay safe.

Woke: Awareness of the issues surrounding racial and social injustice

Conscious: Aware of one's own existence, sensations, thoughts, surroundings etc. **2.** Aware of and responding to ones surroundings; awake **3.** Having knowledge of something; aware **4.** To notice that a particular thing or person exists or is present.

Consciousness The state or quality of awareness, or, of being aware of an external object or something within oneself.

"Knowledge is consciousness of reality"

UNKNOWN

#wakeup
OR
"Smile now, Cry later"

"True philanthropy comes from living from the heart of yourself and giving what you have been given. How will you do that how will you use your personality the energy of your personality to serve that which is your soul's calling? ...Any life and every life is enhanced by the sharing and the giving and the opening up of the hearts space your life gets better when you can find a way to share it with someone else... how will you use yourself, how will you use everything that you have been given to serve that which is greater than yourself?"

Oprah

ABOUT THE AUTHOR

Every melanated person named in this book and every melanated person not in this book that pretty much sums up the author. I am you. Netta B.

"I leave you love. I leave you hope. I leave you the challenge of developing confidence in one another. I leave you respect for the use of power. I leave you faith. I leave you racial dignity."

Mary McLeod Bethune

www.ingramcontent.com/pod-product-compliance
Lightning Source LLC
Chambersburg PA
CBHW070958160426
43193CB00012B/1823